A captivating read for all interested in green business. This book takes a multidisciplinary approach in overviewing Green Business in the 21st century – a must-read for all students of business.

— *Dr. Toni S. Ola. Lecturer in Sustainability and Supply Chain Management, Regent's University London, UK*

Absolute Essentials of Green Business

This short textbook provides a core understanding of the intersection between business and the natural environment. The sector's rapid expansion means that many university programmes are focusing to a greater extent nowadays on the career opportunities generated by the ecological imperative – a curriculum increasingly referred to as "green business". Climate breakdown is a devastating issue facing contemporary society. With six out of the ten largest multinationals listed in the 2018 Fortune Global 500 being active in the energy sector, it is no surprise that more and more business schools are offering modules addressing the management of natural resources. The business world has made some progress incorporating green principles into their strategies and operations, but progress needs to accelerate in line with global agreements to prevent catastrophic ecological and environmental problems. *Absolute Essentials of Green Business* stands out because of its singular focus on a subset of this wider curricular area. By covering both the macro (framework) and micro (business strategy) aspects of the topic, the book's structure is in line with the way modules of this nature are taught in universities today.

Students of business and environmental studies will benefit from reading this concise textbook in order to develop their understanding of a fundamental element of the social science curriculum.

Alan Sitkin is Senior Lecturer in International Business at Regents University, UK.

Absolute Essentials of Business and Economics

Textbooks are an extraordinarily useful tool for students and teachers, as is demonstrated by their continued use in the classroom and online. Successful textbooks run into multiple editions, and in endeavouring to keep up with developments in the field, it can be difficult to avoid increasing length and complexity.

This series of short textbooks offers a range of books which zero-in on the absolute essentials. In focusing on only the core elements of each sub-discipline, the books provide a useful alternative or supplement to traditional textbooks.

Absolute Essentials of Green Business
Alan Sitkin

For more information about this series, please visit: www.routledge.com/Absolute-Essentials-of-Business-and-Economics/book-series/ ABSOLUTE

Absolute Essentials of Green Business

Alan Sitkin

LONDON AND NEW YORK

First published 2020
by Routledge
2 Park Square, Milton Park, Abingdon, Oxon OX14 4RN

and by Routledge
52 Vanderbilt Avenue, New York, NY 10017

Routledge is an imprint of the Taylor & Francis Group, an informa business

© 2020 Alan Sitkin

British Library Cataloguing-in-Publication Data
A catalogue record for this book is available from the British Library

Library of Congress Cataloging-in-Publication Data
A catalog record has been requested for this book

ISBN: 978-0-367-19672-1 (hbk)
ISBN: 978-0-429-20386-2 (ebk)

Typeset in Times New Roman
by codeMantra

Visit the eResources: www.routledge.com/9780367196721

Contents

Foreword   viii

Acknowledgements   x

1   Introduction to green business   1

2   Resource depletion   14

3   Pollution management   27

4   Environmental economics and policies   40

5   Going green: managing the process   52

6   Green operations   63

7   Green marketing   75

8   Green growth sectors   87

9   Clean energy ventures   99

Index   111

Foreword

In recent years, a number of serious and highly competent authors have written books advising companies on how to engage with the ecological challenges facing the world today. Yet for business students seeking to embark on a corporate career, this literature has – on the whole – been of limited use. One reason is because the overwhelming majority of green business books on the market today target current managers rather than students. The present text, on the other hand, is expressly designed as an educational tool helping students to incorporate environmental considerations into their business thinking. Second and above all, with extremely few exceptions today's green business texts exist to communicate devoted environmentalists' visions of what green companies could look like in the future. The problem is that utopian green visions have existed for many years now without most companies implementing the initiatives needed to reshape their activities along greener lines. This new text addresses this dilemma by focusing primarily – and uniquely – on the obstacles hampering companies' transition to a greener future, with consideration also given to potential solutions. However, it is crucial not to repeat the mistake that many worthy green business authors make of confusing hope with reality. Green business can only advance as a discipline if sufficient respect is paid to the factors hindering its development.

Of course, green business authors do deserve full praise for their enthusiasm. The present book wholeheartedly shares their view that an ecological imperative does exist, and that it is incumbent upon all business students to take stock of its implications when planning their future careers. The environmental crisis is very real, and unless it is resolved, nothing else will matter. Yet this dilemma has been widely publicised for many years now. The real question is why companies have been slow to come up with real remedies.

Modern teaching empowers learners by facilitating access to knowledge. Towards that end, Routledge's revolutionary mini-textbook format offers a concise package of all the main green business concepts, separating them from more secondary aspects in order to focus entirely on the core principles underlying this new and evolving discipline. The same directness applies to the learning tools that accompany this work. The book itself is mainly comprised of text (enhanced by graphic vignettes, relevant figures and background references), with other useful features such as indicative online case studies and classroom activities being found on the associated website, to ensure they are updated promptly over time.

Acknowledgements

It is impossible to pay tribute to everyone who influenced me to write a book combining so many strands of my academic, professional, political and personal lives. Clearly my values were first shaped by Dad, who taught me that self-interest is only commendable when aligned with the greater good; and by Mom, who taught me to ask why things are as they are, and whether other possibilities exist. In sharing these paradigms with me, Jim and Susan have always helped me to gauge their application, and for that I will always be grateful. Above and beyond my original family, however, too many other loved ones, friends, acquaintances and indeed adversaries have contributed to my understanding of this world for me to name all of them. So even as I acknowledge a few individuals, my thoughts are also with all those I do not have time to mention here. You know who you are.

Relating more specifically to green business, my first thanks go to Terry Clague at Routledge, who believed in this project from the outset and was, along with his colleague Matt R., incredibly helpful in getting it going. Similar thanks goes to Assunta and her team for all their editing work. Talking about editors, I'd also like to thank Tim Goodfellow for his support with earlier writings in this nascent discipline. Lastly, I'm grateful to mon pote Richard for introducing me to the wonderful Marie Dubois, useful because of her great drawings but also for her creative insights into how readers might view the different topics that the book evokes.

More broadly, I've been lucky to count as friends Achilleas, who has been on both sides of the green and business fences and has fantastic stories about both – and Jayne C., whose collaboration on the municipally owned heat from waste company Energetik that we founded has been priceless.

Above all, my thoughts go to the family I've created. The young German social democrat demonstrating against nuclear power plants in the 1980s? Reader, I married her 36 happy years ago, and long may it last. Having said that, Verena would want me to finish by referring to our kids, if only because they are the future and green business is all about that. So my final thanks are to Lea, one of the kindest persons I've ever known (and a fierce warrior against plastics); and to admirable Dani, who together with Jo inspires me with their fight for baby Leo and all of tomorrow's children. Their collective example proves that the song is correct – the kids are, indeed, alright.

1 Introduction to green business

"$500 notes burn best"

ESSENTIAL SUMMARY

Like any discipline, green business reflects a context that learners would do well to understand before assessing how this new field of study applies to their future professional choices. The first thing that stands out is the multidisciplinary nature of green business, explained in the chapter's initial section through an overview of the historical circumstances guiding its emergence.

(Continued)

Quite unusually for a social discipline, however, green business also has deep roots in natural science, to the extent that it is valuable for learners to re-familiarise themselves with certain basic principles that they will have acquired during their earlier education. Lastly and in line with this book's decision to question why green business has not spread more widely already, the chapter's final section analyses explanations for the corporate world's relative estrangement from environmentalism – the purpose being to determine how this gulf might ultimately be bridged.

Section I. The ecological mindset

Since the dawn of time, most civilisations have struggled to situate humankind's connection to its natural environment. In the prehistoric era, before advances in technology and science created more rational ways of analysing this relationship, the predominant attitude was to fear nature's potential for creating harm (through natural disasters, dangerous wildlife or starvation). Such fears were compounded by general ignorance of the physical processes underlying events over which our ancestors had little if any control. Early animists would often attribute a spirit to a place – its so-called genius loci – and view natural elements as moody gods with the power to either nurture or destroy humankind. Precautionary tales about nature abounded in ancient civilisations, exemplified in Greek mythology by stories about Prometheus or Icarus being punished or killed because they sought, respectively, to steal fire or fly close to the sun. More than living in harmony with the natural world, early populations felt a need to obey it.

Over time, most societies began assuming a more aggressive stance towards nature even as some voices continued to advocate harmonious coexistence. In the Judeo-Christian Bible, this ambivalence is witnessed in the contradictory statements from the book of Genesis that humans should "preserve the land" (2:15) but also "fill the Earth and subdue it" (1:26). Eastern religions also offered mixed messages, with many of Hinduism's Vedic scriptures expressing reverence for the natural world while simultaneously doubting its reality. Without purporting to review the sum total of historical attitudes towards nature, suffice it to say that as different civilisations gained confidence in their ability to control nature, it lost its mystical properties and began to be seen as something that might be instrumentalised – all the more so given the widespread belief in the inexhaustibility of natural resources.

Over time, the combined effects of population growth, industrialisation and resource demand would cause many if not most inhabitants of Planet Earth to take their physical environment for granted. Later this would spawn a counter-reaction that focused, conversely, on the need to protect nature. This latter mindset, known today as ecological thinking, has opened the door to what contemporaries call green business.

It is important to clarify the diverse nature of the various strands comprising ecological thinking. Each has its own background and reflects different sensitivities that can best be understood in the context of the circumstances in which it arose.

Early strands of ecological thinking

It was in 1869, shortly after Charles Darwin published his text on the scientific principles driving the evolution of species, that German philosopher Ernst Haeckel coined the term "ecology", derived from the Greek for house (οικος or *oikos*) and speech (λóγος or *logos*). Thus, ecology involves talking about every aspect of a community's ability to survive in a particular place – an approach that is intentionally holistic and multidisciplinary, with objects of study always being viewed in the context of the many different factors that enable life.

Haeckel was not the first scholar to engage in such thinking, however. In the late 18th century, for instance, the English demographer Thomas Malthus devised a series of laws showing how population growth causes crises due to the competition for finite resources. This paradigm still applies, one example being the link between today's accelerated resource depletion and new demand emerging from many emerging economies. In many cases, ecological distress is still best analysed in population size terms.

Another notable thinker from the early 19th century was German botanist Alexander von Humboldt, who applied rudimentary ecological principles to forestry projects across Latin America and India. It is significant that the countries where Humboldt conducted his experiments were places of great political and economic interest to England and Spain, the colonial powers of the day – an early example of how material interests are as much a driver of scientific study of the natural world as the desire for pure knowledge is. Given the preponderance of agricultural economics during this era, it is also no surprise that Humboldt's discoveries disseminated quickly throughout European farming. Ties between science and business have a long history.

Having said that, the motivation driving many other 19th-century writers with an interest in the environment was not material but spiritual – a mindset that also exists today. In 1854, New England essayist Henry David Thoreau wrote a seminal compilation entitled "Walden" extolling humans living in harmony with nature. Similar attitudes were advocated 40 years later in California by John Muir, explorer of Yosemite Park and founder of the Sierra Club, and in England by the author Beatrix Potter, who purchased large tracts of land in the Lake District to prevent development. Potter's actions exemplified the fears felt by some in Europe and North America that their idyllic countryside was being destroyed by factories, denounced by the poet William Blake as "satanic mills". Vestiges of this attitude can be seen in certain modern land planning laws, including "green belt" restrictions limiting growth on metropolitan peripheries.

The first half of the 20th century was an industrial era marked by the rise of Fordist mass production and consumption. There were a few notable ecologists, like US President Theodore Roosevelt, whose administration created his country's first national parks. By and large, however, the environment was a peripheral issue in most societies at the time, especially in countries at the earlier stages of industrial development – an international differentiation marking green business studies to this day. One poignant example is Russia's old Soviet regime, which in its rush to conquer a vast territory undertook the astounding step of reversing the direction of major rivers to enhance their economic utility. Another was the uncontrolled deforestation of vast swathes of Latin America and Asia – following a pattern of poor soil practice long witnessed in the older industrialised countries (exemplified in the 1930s by the Oklahoma "Dust Bowl"). All in all, this was an era when economic development tended to supersede ecological priorities most everywhere.

The rise of mass environmentalism

Improved economic well-being during much of the late 20th century coincided with growing acceptance of an ecological imperative. Such changes raise questions about the extent to which a green mindset derives from a "social ecology" reaction to environmental imperatives – a mindset grounded in science and real social–political interactions – or from a "deep ecology" stance rooted in a quasi-religious attitude. The debate continues even today (Figure 1.1).

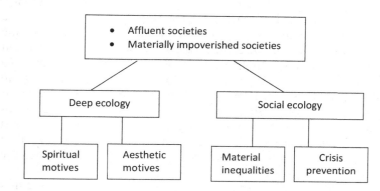

Figure 1.1 Different Strands of the Ecological Mindset.

The social ecology approach can be witnessed in the chain of events that followed the mid-20th century "Green Revolution" that used technology to increase agricultural productivity. A key element of this agenda was the introduction of pesticides such as Dichlorodiphenyltrichloroethane (DDT) that seriously damaged water systems (and bird populations) worldwide. The rising volume of industrial effluents was having the same effect, one notorious case being Japan's Minamata Bay disaster, where mercury outflows from a local factory poisoned local fish stocks, increasing cancer rates and the number of children born with deformities. The end result was the 1962 publication of a book that became a seminal work for the global environmental movement: *Silent Spring*, written by the American marine biologist Rachel Carson. The resonance of this text was such that governments worldwide started establishing quality authorities and enacting legislation meant to change business practices. One direct effect was that many chemical companies began researching new ways of increasing crop yields. Within a few decades, this would contribute to the development of genetically modified (GM) organisms, becoming in time another topic of controversy for environmentalists. The lesson from this chain of events is that much in the same way that environmentalists highlight the interdependency of natural processes, there is also an ecological relationship between the different business, political and social forces whose actions affect the environment. Ecology is as much as social science as a natural one.

It was towards the late 1960s and early 1970s that the global environmental movement finally achieved self-awareness. Professors at the

University of California, Santa Barbara, having witnessed the devastation wreaked on the local coastline by an oil spill in 1969, launched one of the world's first environmental studies programmes. The economic foundations for this new discipline were laid in seminal texts produced by a new vanguard of scholars. These included Garrett Hardin's *The Tragedy of the Commons* (1968), Paul Ehrlich's *The Population Bomb* (1968) and E. F. Schumacher's *Small Is Beautiful: Economics As If People Mattered* (1973). Some observers also trace this rise in environmental awareness to Apollo moon flight images taken of a beautiful but vulnerable Planet Earth – imagery that sparked a famous 1972 treatise by British scientist James Lovelock, "Gaia as seen through the atmosphere".

The sum total of this corpus meant that by the mid-1970s, ecologists had the intellectual means to sustain a vocal constituency. The activist organisation Greenpeace, founded in Canada in 1972, launched several high-profile campaigns (against nuclear testing and commercial whaling), operating alongside older groups such as World Wildlife Fund (1961) and Friends of the Earth (1969).

At first, these movements barely echoed in the general public. Interest in the environment, crystallising in events like the first "Earth Day" organised on 22 April 1970, seemed largely confined to marginal or academic constituencies. Several governments began to diffuse environmental messages – one example being a campaign launched in France during the 1970s asking citizens to "hunt down waste" (*chasse au gaspi*) and reduce the mountains of litter plaguing the country's landscape. Large-scale efforts of this kind were few and far between, however.

The same apathy continued into the early 1980s, an era whose predominant zeitgeist is often deemed to have prioritised individualism and material welfare, famously encapsulated in the dictum from Oliver Stone's emblematic film *Wall Street* that "greed is good" – a philosophy diametrically opposed to the abnegation that is one pillar of much ecological thinking. Similarly, many economies like India, China and Brazil that are in the process of emerging today were still suffering from abject poverty at the time – meaning their main priorities were material, with environmentalism generally viewed as irrelevant (and possibly provocative).

By the late 1980s, however, there were clear signs in many countries that green thinking was starting to go mainstream. One indicator was the growing number of politicians seeking to co-opt environmental ideas, often for electoral purposes but also because a series of disasters over the previous 15 years had convinced many of the need to finally face up to the problem. In Germany, the world had already witnessed the first serious attempt by a green movement to gain political power. "Die Grüne", originally led by Petra Kelly and Joschka Fischer, was born out of anti-nuclear power demonstrations in cities like Hamburg that had earned much publicity and admiration worldwide. At a transnational level, 1987 saw both the Brundtland Commission's seminal report enshrining the concept of "sustainable development" and the Montreal Protocol's restrictions on further use of harmful chlorofluorocarbon (CFC) compounds creating holes in the Earth's ozone layer. This latter action had a decisive effect on the industrial activities of refrigerator manufacturers worldwide. It is also one of the first examples of a global policy, driven by actors' sense of the ecological imperative, constraining companies' room to manoeuvre while creating opportunities for commercial expansion (substances replacing the noxious CFCs).

Another key factor was accelerating globalisation. This had a contradictory effect, with the explosion in world trade increasing demands on planetary resources even as the concomitant rise in information exchanges spread global environmental consciousness. Such awareness would disseminate further through the efforts of the "eco-pedagogy" movement that the Brazilian educator Paolo Freire founded in the wake of the UN's 1992 Rio Earth Summit, based on the idea that all academic learning needed to be rooted in ecological thinking because the impossibility of material happiness meant there was no other alternative. This new value system, diametrically opposed to the one conveyed in traditional corporate marketing campaigns, would pave the way for the rise of "social marketing", one category of which became "green marketing".

By the 2000s, most societies worldwide featured active green lobbies whose words and deeds resonated throughout the media. Embodied in global benchmarks like the United Nations Sustainable Development Goals, environmentalism is a bona fide social and political aspiration today – as well as an integral part of the corporate social responsibility (CSR) agenda to which many companies adhere. The recurrence of ecological disasters – like Hurricane Katrina that devastated New Orleans in 2005, the red toxic sludge that overwhelmed the Hungarian town of Kolontar in 2010 or 2018's record global summer heat wave – has convinced more and more citizens worldwide to view ecological breakdown as an absolute imperative. The question then becomes whether business feels the same (Figure 1.2).

Year (s)	Country/region	Incident	Description
1960s onwards	Soviet Union	Aral Sea	Destruction of lake due to water diversion
1976	Italy	Seveso	Plant explosion causing cloud of toxic dioxins
1978	France	Amoco Cadiz	Oil tanker spilling ca.1.6m barrels on Brittany shores
1976–1978	US	Love Canal	Chemical dumpsite, health hazard for local residents
1979	US	Three Mile Island	Nuclear plant leaks
1980s	Global, esp. Australia	Ozone layer	Increased solar radiation causing rise in skin cancer
1984	India	Bhopal	Chemical plant explosion, thousands of deaths
1986	Ukraine	Chernobyl	Nuclear plant explosion
1989	US	Exxon Valdez	Oil tanker spilling ca.1.2m barrels on Alaska shores
1997	Asia	Smog cloud	Deforestation fires cause 3200 km long air hazard
1990s	Europe	BSE	Mad cow disease, herd slaughters, human deaths
2000s	US (Louisiana)	- Hurricane Katrina - Gulf of Mexico	- Devastates New Orleans - BP oil spill
2010s	Japan	Fukushima	Tsunami wrecks nuclear plant, radioactivity spreads

Figure 1.2 Recent Ecological Disasters Sharpening Green Sensitivities.

Section II. Basic science for managers

At one level, green business seeks to overcome the centuries-long estrangement between economics and ecology by asserting the inter-dependency between the two – a linkage famously expressed in the concept of "natural capitalism". It remains that this re-connection will only take root if all managers – and not just R&D or manufacturing specialists – are equipped to integrate ecological principles into their business decisions. The first step towards empowering managers with this capability is to ensure a wider diffusion of relevant knowledge.

Green business and general scientific principles

Biology features many elements relevant to future managers' green business decision-making. At an applied level, the concept of "bio-utilisation" speaks to new uses of organisms as raw materials, exemplified by plant-based plastics. Analogous concepts such as "biomimicry" refer to the use of enhanced design to create goods with properties imitating the natural world. These approaches are part of a general search for sustainability in the original sense of this term, i.e. the capacity of organisms (or ecosystems) to self-perpetuate. Species' ultimate survival depends on their evolutionary ability to defend themselves against external risks. For companies, this means integrating sustainability mechanisms into operations and getting feedback from the outside world to ensure that progress is being made. The processes are modelled after the life cycles that species and ecosystems develop to survive – including by using the end-of-life of some organisms as a means for sustaining others.

Environmental chemistry involves all of the molecular interactions affecting land, sea and atmospheric systems – first and foremost being photosynthesis, the process by means of which sunlight is converted into a sugar called adenosine triphosphate (ATP) that stores the chemical energy underlying the food chains that nurture all flora (hence fauna) on Earth. Chemistry is also key to pollution studies. Industrial waste is a real health hazard for humans, fauna and flora. Few industrial systems are self-contained i.e. they produce waste that seeps into the surrounding environment. Because of this, it is critical that managers gain a basic understanding of green chemistry either to minimise their outputs' negative impacts (i.e. by generating only biodegradable waste) or else to enhance their inputs' quality (i.e. by prioritising organic over synthetic compounds).

Environmental physics also offer managers powerful green business applications. All human activity draws upon energy resources and is only worthwhile insofar as the outputs have greater value than the inputs. This calculation is complicated by Newton's second law of entropy postulating that some of the energy transferred during a physical operation is necessarily wasted, often in the form of heat. Unless this "heat waste" is re-captured, other energy inputs must be found to fuel future operations. Clearly, the more efficient an operation (i.e. the less heat it wastes or the more heat it re-captures), the less it requires additional energy inputs. The greater productivity of eco-efficient operations explains the business world's growing interest in closed-loop systems (buildings, industrial processes, etc.) that maximise the recycling hence conservation of energy.

Earth sciences

There are several ways in which water sciences (including hydrology and oceanography) interest environmentally minded managers. Because water is essential to all life on Earth, humankind has always been focused on it. The infrastructure implications are enormous. There is also great interest in the role that water systems play in shaping land masses through processes like erosion, subsidence or the flows of nutrients or sediments. Otherwise, with fertiliser nitrates increasingly running off to create oxygen-deprived "dead zones" in many coastal waters – and given global warming's negative impact on agricultural productivity – there is growing interest in "aquaculture" or the practice of growing in water organisms that can be used for food (and potentially for energy) purposes.

Just as important is geology, or the study of the Earth's surface, together with its main adjuncts: rock and mineral formations; and crop and soil management. The first category provides knowledge that can be of critical value in sectors like energy (i.e. petroleum, natural gas and coal); mining (i.e. minerals like bauxite for aluminium, iron for steel, copper for wiring or silicon for conductivity; elements like chlorine for industrial cleansing, or uranium for nuclear fission); and construction (buildings safe from subsidence or earthquakes). As for crop and soil management, this is first and foremost of importance to managers in agribusiness, a sector destined to account for a larger percentage of future global economic activity as supply/demand imbalances cause foodstuffs' relative price to rise compared with manufactured goods or services.

Lastly, business managers are increasingly affected by the science of climatology and/or its short-term weather-focused variant, meteorology. The starting point here is solar radiation. When sunlight is converted into energy following photosynthesis and stored in plants, it becomes a primary fuel source for all life on Earth, either directly as biomass or indirectly after decomposing into fossil fuels. Nor should it be forgotten that solar radiation is the Earth's only source of heat. Until recently, this heat would dissipate into outer space at a rate moderating temperatures across much of the planet, thereby enabling our global civilisation to flourish. With greenhouse gases accumulating in the outer atmosphere, this dissipation mechanism has weakened. The net effect is that ambient temperatures are trending sharply upwards, with potentially devastating consequences for all life on Earth.

Section III. Management's historical estrangement from environmentalism

It is one thing to use scientific principles to explain to managers the usefulness of acquiring environmental knowledge. It is another to ask why green business has not developed even more quickly than it has. As aforementioned, the principles underlying environmental science have been widely known for centuries. Newspapers abound today with stories of the bottom-line benefits for companies of going green, whether this involves processes, products or reputation. Given economists' presumption that people make rational decisions in most circumstances, one would expect managers paid for their forward thinking to have long made a core corporate function out of environmentalism. Discovering why this has not happened is a good starting point for determining under what conditions it might in the future.

One of the key premises underlying this book is that companies' initial turn towards green business is almost always time-consuming and, above all, expensive, especially if the environmentals efforts involve replacing tried and tested sunk investments with costly and relatively untested green assets, technologies or practices. Since competitive pressures may prevent these heavy upfront costs from being passed on to customers, going green may reduce earnings in the short run – with some managers not being willing to take the risk that this investment, like any other, might ultimately not pay for itself.

In addition, few companies have had to bear the full cost of their activities' negative externalities until now, with the rest of society carrying the burden of whatever pollution they produce or resources they deplete. Companies would lose this advantage if their environmental footprint were fully internalised and costed. Similarly, some managers will hesitate to assume the costs of going green if they expect the benefits of such actions to accrue to society as a whole – disdain for enabling "free riders" is a powerful emotion in much modern business. And there will be others questioning whether it is a good idea to take on the costs of going green if their rivals do not do the same.

Another kind of analysis can be found in the body of management literature that analyses how the relationship between business owners and corporate managers has varied over time. Part of this corpus discusses how the growth of huge, multidivisional corporations during the early 20th century gave birth to a class of mobile managers who did not necessarily have the same concern for a local community's environmental or other well-being as local managers were likely to have. The strong intimation here is that anonymous institutional investors' overriding focus on financial returns undermine any real environmental sensitivity.

An ancillary analysis also best understood in an international business framework is the temptation for some multinational enterprises (MNEs) to play one government against another when making investment location decisions. This kind of "regime shopping", made possible because of the asymmetrical power relationship between mobile MNEs and territorially bound national governments, may create situations forcing a country to "race to the bottom", lowering its environmental standards because the associated costs render it less attractive to footloose MNEs.

A final international business-related impediment has been the widespread dismantling of trade barriers over the past 40 years. This has led to an expansion in cross-border trade: between firms, but also within them (with an estimated 60 percent of all trade today comprised of intra-firm flows). Applying classical theories of national specialisation and comparative advantage, many MNEs have sought to maximise plant-level economies of scale by splitting global production between distant specialist factories, each focused on a particular stage of the manufacturing process (components, assembly, etc.). This fragmentation makes sense at a corporate level as long as the logistics costs associated with all these inter-subsidiary flows remain low. However, it has also led to an explosion in global demand for energy, due to the intense logistics associated with this extensive spatial organisation but also because many manufacturing activities have been offshored to emerging economies where environmentalism may be viewed as less of a priority than escaping poverty through economic development.

Last but not least, a new activity like green business constitutes by definition a change in the way most companies have been run historically. It therefore faces the same obstacles as any other change driver, with many managers' conservatively perceiving their interest to be preserving tried and test routines instead of adopting new ones. People bring their individual opinions to the workplace, and with some managers remaining unconvinced of the ecological imperative – and others daunted by the scale of the challenge, preferring ostrich-like procrastination – it can be very difficult for environmental activists to bring colleagues on board. They will often be derided as troublesome doomsayers, a sentiment that diminishes the general sense of urgency and feeds into the idea that green business need not be considered in any great depth until some unspecified time in the future. Even as this book rejects suicidally myopic attitudes of this kind, it also refuses to lull students (future managers and executives) into a false sense of complacency by exaggerating how widespread green business has actually become. The reality is that the vast majority of companies are already very aware of the ecological imperative yet truly struggle to embrace it fully. The question then becomes why they find this so daunting. It is only by understanding their apprehension that it might ultimately be overcome.

Bibliography

Brundtland, G. (1987), "Report of the World Commission on Environment and Development: Our Common Future", United Nations Document, Transmitted to the General Assembly as an Annex to document A/42/427 – Development and International Co-operation: Environment.

Freeman, R. and McVea, J. (1984), "A stakeholder approach to strategic management", Darden University of Virginia Working Paper no. 01-02.

Lovelock, J. (2–5 June 1982), "Gaia as seen through the atmosphere", Biological and Geological Perspectives Paper presented at the Fourth International Symposium on Biomineralization, Renesse, The Netherlands.

Speth, J. (2003), "The Global Environmental Agenda: Origins and Prospects", http://environment.yale.edu/publication-series/documents/downloads/o-u/speth.pdf

Vogel, D. (2005), *The Market for Virtue: The Potential and Limits of Corporate Social Responsibility*, Brookings Institution Press, Washington DC.

2 Resource depletion

"At least we're getting somewhere. They're just burning fuel"

ESSENTIAL SUMMARY

Physical economic activities have traditionally been organised in a linear fashion, with resources that start as raw materials being accessed and then transformed into outputs which include both desired products and undesired waste. This architecture relies on three conditions: the ability to source inputs; their price; and the hope that the market (and more broadly, society)

(Continued)

welcomes the outputs. The present chapter will analyse the first stage of this process, namely the availability of resources. The book's next chapter will then look at one aspect of its second stage, specifically the treatment of unwanted outputs known as pollution. These two topics embody the main challenges that modern green business purports to address.

Resource availability depends on many variables, starting with the total stock of the raw material in question but also the price at which it can be accessed. Clearly, these two factors are interrelated, with materials whose supply diminishes as stocks deplete – an inevitable outcome with finite natural resources – bound to become more expensive. Now, classical economic assumptions of rationality predict that demand will decline for goods whose price rises, motivating buyers to find a substitute. In reality, some resources have become indispensable to modern industry, with such enormous sums having been sunk into input-specific infrastructure (national electricity grids, internal combustion engines, gas-fired power plants, etc.) that system re-engineering seems prohibitively expensive.

The end result is inertia: business has generally been very slow in responding to resource depletion challenges; and many managers seek to avoid the cost of adaptation during their own careers, passing the problem onto to future generations. Yet indications are that resource depletion constitutes a clear and present danger for companies today. The question is not whether green business should formulate a response to the crisis but how to manage the financial implications of change that is inevitable.

Section I. Energy

There is a strong case to be made that energy derived from natural resources – the main topic in contemporary resource depletion analysis – also constitutes the chief interface between business and environmentalism. Two key factors in this relationship are technology and demand, the latter largely a function of population size and disposable income. In older agricultural economies, most energy came from what has been called "current sunlight", with people eating living plants, using them for building materials or else feeding them to animals that they would then eat or use for clothing. One body of analysis holds that as technological know-how advanced to allow humankind to access "ancient sunlight" stored underground in the form of fossil fuels from dead plants, people were able to access much greater quantities of energy and sustain larger populations. The ensuing demographic growth could only be sustained, however, by drawing upon fossil fuel reserves that were by definition finite in nature and would therefore necessarily be exhausted after years of extraction and consumption. Until the relationship between population growth and greater consumption of finite energy resources is broken, it is impossible to see how these two antinomic trends can continue to co-exist over the long run.

Global energy supply, demand and cost factors

Some factors affecting the future of energy supplies are specific to this one topic. Others relate to long-term societal trends where the availability of power is taken for granted – an assumption that is likely to evaporate as the effects of resource depletion hit home.

At the turn of the 2020s decade, there seems to be a universal consensus that global primary energy consumption is destined to increase for years to come. A leading factor in this outlook is skyrocketing demand from emerging economic powerhouses in the Global South. Because energy elasticity remains high in these countries, rapid marginal gross domestic product (GDP) and population growth – and rising levels of material well-being – has had a disproportionate effect on global demand. Despite some commendable national and corporate sustainability ambitions, the general state of technology in many emerging economies translates into comparatively energy-intensive manufacturing processes, especially in low-margin firms lacking the financial resources to invest in greener technology. Thus, as globalisation forces shift manufacturing away from the Global North, overall energy usage is expected to continue to rise. This is especially true due to the internationalisation of many multinational companies' supply chains, with growing volumes of intermediary materials, components and modules manufactured in distant specialist locations before being transported to their final assembly or sales locations – shipments that themselves consume great quantities of energy.

A second explanation for predicted rises in global energy demand can be found in the behaviour of many Global North citizens, encapsulated in a phenomenon commonly referred to as Jevon's Paradox. This idea is based on the empirical observation that societies whose technological capabilities enable greater energy efficiency tend in actual fact to increase their total consumption, largely because actors start assuming that the modern equipment they use is more efficient and therefore make less of an effort to conserve and/or not waste energy. It is a finding that also points to the importance of other more psychological factors affecting modern civilisation's response (or lack thereof) to the resource depletion crisis. Data has shown, for instance, relatively little correlation in recent decades between energy prices and consumption. In terms of business behaviour – and in addition to the aforementioned discussion about people feeling daunted by the scale of the challenge – this inelasticity reflects some managers' inability or unwillingness to process and act upon available information about resource depletion, intimating in turn that much thinking in this area is guided more by institutional influences than by rational strategizing. Otherwise, many managers (and indeed, consumers) seem prepared to accept regular small increases in energy prices, driving steadily upwards the threshold beyond which they might start to seek substitutes. Gradual bad news tends to spark less of a reaction than sudden emergencies. Like all economics, green business is also contingent on subjectivity phenomena.

Having said that, other factors affecting the availability and price of (hence demand for) energy are more objective in nature. The discussion here starts with the fact that around 35 percent of primary global energy sources are expended on the infrastructure required to access and distribute energy from its original production locations – oil platform, gas field, coalmine, nuclear power plant – to the innumerable locations worldwide where it is consumed. The actual percentage of energy expended on energy distribution depends on the mode involved (tanker, pipeline, liquefaction and above all electrical power lines) and is predicted to fall over time as technology improves – one example being the way in which future electric power lines will be able to function over longer distances using high voltage direct current. This will remain a fundamental problem for the foreseeable future, however, given that the main regions where energy is produced tend to be very distant from the places where most is consumed. One response that could get energy savings and safety concerns to align might be to use new small-scale micro-generation solutions that maximise the consumption of locally produced fuels. The problem here is that the smaller size of facilities serving smaller local populations precludes their achieving the same economies of scale as today's larger more centralised power plants. Less energy would be lost to (and spent on) energy distribution but the per-unit cost of energy production is also higher.

Lastly, it is also worth noting the breakdown in global primary energy consumption by user type. This is important because user categories can vary markedly in both consumption and energy intensity terms. One example is the expected rapid rise over the coming decades in transportation-related energy consumption (led by the ongoing expansion in aviation). This differs from the outlook for residential and commercial lighting, which should benefit greatly from the advent of new LED technologies. Similarly, the main energy consumption modes also vary globally, reflecting factors such as regional variations in climate (thus heating needs), agricultural patterns or industrial specialisation. There is a tendency for many businesses to conceptualise energy supplies in the light of their own electricity provision – the most common form of energy today (and increasingly so given the predicted demise in fossil fuels and introduction of electric automobiles) – but the big picture is that the global energy market constitutes a patchwork of fuel sources and uses.

Main energy categories

Among conventional sources, fossil fuels currently account altogether for more than three-quarters of total energy consumption. At the same time, two of these fuels (oil and natural gas) are currently predicted by leading professional sources (like the BP Global Energy Outlook and the United National Environment Programme) to be entirely exhausted in around a half-century. With coal reserves only expected to last about one century at current consumption rates (and with the same applying to uranium ore feeding the world's nuclear plants), the world faces a situation where almost all the energy sources currently powering human civilisation are due to deplete in the lifetime of generations already born today. By itself, this renders knowledge of energy supply a crucial capability for all managers, especially those seeking a career in green business.

Before exploring the specificities of the three hydrocarbon fossil fuels driving today's economy (oil, natural gas and coal), it is worth remembering the price correlation between them, particularly the first two. On the production side, natural gas is often a by-product of oil exploration. On the demand side, a visible substitution effect exists between these two resources, with higher oil prices tending to spark increased demand for natural gas, thus higher prices for the latter. The two markets are not entirely parallel, since oil prices are more or less set on a global basis, whereas the gas trade tends to be more regional due to this fuel's particular transportation constraints (somewhat alleviated by the recent rise of liquefied natural gas). Otherwise, it is worth noting the much more localised nature of the market for coal, whose pricing structure is more closely linked to national factors such as seam depth, extraction methods and logistics. As oil and gas prices rise over time, the costs of liquefying coal will also become increasingly justifiable. Facilitating the distribution of a particular fuel type turns it into a more viable direct substitute for its counterparts.

Oil

As aforementioned, energy demand is predicted to continue growing rapidly in the decades to come, especially as economic development continues apace in the Global South. On the supply side, efforts to increase global capacities are expected to alleviate short-term pressures to some small extent, especially as higher prices render exploration more viable in otherwise uneconomic environments. It remains that all market participants acknowledge the ultimate depletion of this finite resource, even before taking into account policies likely to be adopted the light of the impending global warming crisis, as discussed in this book's next chapter (Figure 2.1).

Current oil supply volumes are complicated by issues relating to national storage policies; the different speeds at which natural gas can be liquefied into oil equivalent products; spare drilling capacities in leading producer nations (reflecting policy decisions about how quickly oil should be extracted from existing fields at a given moment in time); and global refining capacities, determining the amount of crude that can be actually distilled into usable oil-based products. Existing institutional and infrastructural mechanisms are likely to keep oil price rises reasonably orderly over the short run. Whether this makes good business sense remains to be seen, however. By masking the signals that would otherwise give companies a rational sense of the urgency of preparing for tomorrow's post-oil world, a temporary calm in oil price setting mechanisms lulls managers into a false sense of complacency and de-incentivises rational behaviour. When viewed in this light, green business is the only variant that makes economic sense.

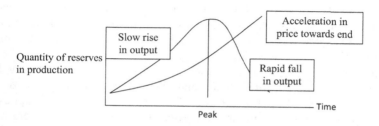

Figure 2.1 Hubbert's Peak Oil Construct.

Natural gas

In addition to the discovery of a few large new fields worldwide, the main discussion as regards this source of energy is the recent development of "fracking", a technique for tapping natural gas from shale rock. Shale gas is very rich in organic material and will add to natural gas reserves in several countries worldwide for several decades to come. The main problem is that processing this new source generates enormous quantities of greenhouse gas emissions. Natural gas itself may be "cleaner" than oil but it too can aggravate climate change dynamics if derived from shale (or from underwater frozen methane hydrate gas deposits, as Japan has sought to do).

For the moment, however, there is no doubt that all this exploratory drilling for shale has had a direct effect on energy prices – lowering them temporarily but dramatically in countries like the USA where the technology is already widespread. Europe presents an interesting case study at this level, with great business interest in certain energy-hungry but resource-poor countries like Germany or the UK but also strong political resistance due to the fuel source's environmental impacts. It will be instructive to see how this stand-off plays out in the years to come, given many European nations' commitment to phasing out "dirty coal" and replacing it with renewables – not to mention a broad interest in tapping into domestic gas sources instead of relying on external delivery mechanisms (often involving Russia, with all the geopolitical risks this entails). The green business lesson here is that the demand for (and supply of) any particular energy source depends not only on variables inherent to the item itself but also on external factors and indeed arbitrage possibilities with other fuel types.

Coal

Although coal, as aforementioned, has a lower production-to-reserves ratio than its fellow fossil fuels, the market has recently been subjected to severe price pressures due to skyrocketing demand in China, where the energy generation apparatus tends to be dominated by this one commodity.

One salient characteristic of the coal market is its great price volatility. This makes it difficult to generalise about demand behaviour, hence depletion scenarios, for coal. Clearly, coal's relative cheapness and abundance have made it the energy of choice for many emerging industrial nations. The extent of any one country's affinity for it will depend, however, on attitudes towards the ecological imperative. Because burning coal produces so much CO_2, countries where pollution considerations outweigh economic concerns will try as far as possible to avoid it – at least until real progress is achieved in carbon capture and storage technology. As other fossil fuels become less plentiful, however, there is a risk that the current disaffection for coal will change.

Nuclear

Until a few short years ago, devoted environmentalists were united in their opposition to atomic fission as an energy source, due to justifiable fears about the dangers of radioactivity (the so-called zero or infinity arbitrage between the low risk of an accident occurring and the devastating effects were it to happen). Nuclear power has also been widely criticised due to the expense of building safe reactors, with cost calculations often neglecting nuclear plants' end-of-life decommissioning. Such criticisms remain well-founded, but there has been a sea change in attitudes towards the nuclear industry: because general energy depletion concerns have sparked fears of impending fuel shortages; because the climate change crisis puts a premium on fuels like nuclear that do not emit greenhouse gases; and because safer and more energy-efficient reactors are constantly being developed. As a result, some governments that had hesitated to increase the role of nuclear in their energy mix have changed policy. Others, on the other hand, frightened by the Fukuyama reactor meltdown in Japan in 2011, have taken the opposite course.

Nuclear power's part in future global energy supplies is bound to be patchy, however. The technology is not distributed evenly across the world, with attempts by certain non-nuclear nations to build reactors often being opposed for geopolitical reasons. Otherwise, green sensitivities to nuclear continue to vary enormously, Of course, the outlook for nuclear could change dramatically if scientists ever developed waste-free "fusion" processes that use a variety of fuels such as deuterium, lithium or magnesium, whose reserves are almost infinite. The problem is that generating energy generation in this way (imitating the processes that power the sun) remains more science fiction than fact.

Section II. Non-energy resources

One way of categorising non-energy resources feeding directly into corporate industrial cycles is to divide them between minerals and biological substances. With respect to the former, this is a category that is worth studying less due to specific depletion concerns and more because most mineral commodities lend themselves to the kinds of conservation and recycling activities that would have the effect, when generalised throughout a company's physical operations, of reducing overall resource consumption. As for biological resources, this is a topic that can be discussed both in the present chapter covering resource depletion and in the following one covering pollution, given the connection between these two problems where living organisms are concerned.

Industrial mineral resources

Information about global mineral deposits is generally less comprehensive than data on global energy reserves. This is probably because the depletion scenarios applicable to many of the minerals used in modern industrial processes run into several hundreds of years instead of a few short decades. At some abstract level, it is true that minerals are also finite, non-renewable commodities that are just as vulnerable to over-consumption as energy resources. This is less of a problem with minerals, however, since most can be recycled and reused relatively easily. The main question here is the economics of such operations, which will depend on factors like the qualities of a particular mineral (weight, propensity) or its ease of transportation. With gold, for instance, almost all of the ore that has ever been mined remains in circulation. As for copper, this mineral is often smelted together with other substances but usually retains enough value to be worth recovering as scrap. Chromium, on the other hand, can lose some of its structural integrity when used in an industrial process and therefore trades at a discount when it comes in recycled form. In other words, one of the key determinants of mineral resources' availability is the arbitrage between the cost of sourcing new ore versus the cost of organising reverse logistics and reprocessing products through such channels – a calculation complicated by certain industries' habit of promoting planned obsolescence in their products.

Minerals can be divided into metals and non-metallic resources. The latter category is the more abundant and includes all kinds of minerals commonly used in agricultural or chemical industries, including calcium, potassium, sulphur and nitrates, as well as clay and sand resources used for building materials. There is one metallic mineral that enjoys similar abundance – iron, the leading metal in industrial processes such as steel-making and an element that can be used by itself or else in an alloy together with metals like manganese, cobalt and nickel.

Asides from iron, the other geo-chemically "abundant" metals – i.e. that account for more than 0.1 percent of the weight of the Earth's crust – are aluminium, manganese, titanium and magnesium (with many experimental scientists hoping to use the latter to spark nuclear fusion-based power generation). As for geochemically scarce metals, these include copper, lead, zinc, gold, silver and platinum. Some analysts are concerned that supplies of this latter group will be unable to match the rising demand, especially copper and platinum, prime inputs in expanding sectors like construction and transportation (used, respectively, for wiring or for catalytic converters and hydrogen fuel cells).

In a market as internationalised as metals – which is often characterised by great distances between production and consumption locations (mines and markets) – adjusting production to inventory or demand levels can be very difficult. Thus, a company's direct access to mineral resources is largely a reflection of its supply chain positioning. This depends in turn on two factors. First, companies with sufficient financial capabilities may seek to secure their mineral inputs by engaging in upstream ("backwards") vertical integration, i.e. purchasing their own suppliers – in this case, mining companies – to avoid having to source inputs externally. A prime example is the recent flood of Chinese industrialists acquiring mines in Africa. Second, some metals can only be mined in very few locations, meaning that their producers will enjoy a quasi-monopoly. One example here is the new market for so-called rare earth minerals like dysprosium, terbium and neodymium, key substances that can be used as magnets in military applications but also in green products like generators for wind turbines or engines for hybrid cars. Another rare earth is lanthanum, a useful substance for electric batteries that are destined to become an increasingly important fuel source as global oil resources deplete. Indeed, a technological battle has broken out over which mineral should set the standard for new generations of batteries expected to hit the markets over the next few years – viewed all around as an exciting new green business opportunity.

Biological resources

As discussed in Chapter 1, analysing natural resources in ecological terms means viewing them in light of the processes sustaining their life cycles. For many resources, an approach of this kind will centre on very long-term evolutions (formation of fossil fuels, mineral ores deposits, etc.) that may seem of little immediate interest to managers. On the other hand, where companies are directly dependent on resources shaped by biological processes, the health of the ecosystem is of prime importance.

One leading resource in this category is water, which companies use in many different ways: as a fluid to cool machinery; as a vessel to carry off unwanted by-products and dilute noxious effluents; as a cleaning agent; as a foodstuff, etc. Water management can, of course, be analysed from a resource perspective, insofar as human economic activity is often at fault for the depletion of water sources. This can be a consequence of indirect actions (i.e. climate change shrinking glaciers or causing drought) or direct ones (i.e. overuse of finite water sources).

Other leading biological resources risking depletion are elements fitting into different species' food chains. A prime example at this level is provided by the fish in the sea, whose stock is dwindling rapidly following long years of overfishing and the pollution of marine habitats. Efforts to improve the situation – for instance, by replacing wild species such as tuna with farmed fish – can create ancillary problems relating to stocks' health and food chains. The lesson at this level is that once an ecological balance has been disturbed, solutions must address the root cause of the problem rather than its manifestations. The difficulty is that the latter often seems easier to address than the former.

Finally, it is worth studying in detail one biological resource – forestry products (i.e. wood) – that has value for companies both in and of itself and also due to its effects on surrounding ecospheres. Forests are an ecosystem unto themselves, embodying biodiversity principles by providing a habitat and nutrients for other flora (and usually fauna, including pollinating bees) that in turn help trees to sustain their own regeneration cycles. Removing any one participant from this overall process raises a serious risk of undermining an equilibrium that will often have taken millions of years to evolve. It is therefore no surprise that many leading environmentalists have looked to forestry for first-order principles; nor that one of the main sustainability of non-governmental organisations (NGOs) to cooperate with managers worldwide is the Forest Stewardship Council (FSC) (www.fsc.org).

Humans have used wood for millennia for a variety of purposes: as biomass to be burned for heating or power purposes; as material for construction; to make products like paper, etc. Most temperate regions (in Western Europe and the USA, for instance) used to be almost entirely covered with trees. Forest depletion goes back many centuries and has been a major contributor to climate change. In and of itself, burning trees would be carbon neutral if new specimens were planted to replace older ones (with the CO_2 emitted by the former being sucked in by the latter). Due to the historical absence of sustainable forest stewardship, however, many more trees have been cut down over the years than the numbers replaced. This imbalance has accelerated in recent decades as industrialised logging companies attack dense tropical forests located in equatorial regions like the Brazilian Amazon or Indonesia. The scale of this activity is so great that many scientists fear it will send overall climate change past the "tipping point" where global warming becomes irreversible – as exemplified most poignantly by the desertification of parts of the Amazon basin itself. This explains the increasing number of international policy initiatives (cf. http://www.un-redd.org/) aimed at slowing and even reversing the trend towards forest depletion. Governments are very aware of the ecological danger of continuing the current trajectory and have established a series of mechanisms that either compensate Global South countries where logging is most prevalent or encourage the replanting of trees in the Global North. For many communities, trees are big business.

At a more practical level, companies (and consumers) are complicit in the depletion of wood resources when they purchase products associated with unsustainable forestry practices. The current consensus is that it is ecologically healthier to only use wood from fast-growing trees planted in "nursery forests" specifically designed for regular logging and re-growth – the idea being that older forests, which are usually accompanied by dense undergrowth, are carbon-rich and should be left untouched. To promote this policy, the FSC has devised a certification system attesting to the origin of different wood supplies. What remains to be seen is whether an initiative of this kind can suffice to prevent depletion and save ecosystems that continue to be coveted for their industrial value in a world characterised by a growing population of citizens hungry for material resources.

Bibliography

BP (2018), "Statistical Review of World Energy", https://www.bp.com/content/dam/bp/en/corporate/pdf/energy-economics/statistical-review/bp-stats-review-2018-full-report.pdf – renewed every year in June.

Diamond, J. (2005), *Collapse: How Societies Choose to Fail or Survive*, Penguin, London.

Hartmann, T. (2009), *The Last Hours of Ancient Sunlight: Waking Up to Personal and Global Transformation*, Hodder & Stoughton, London.

Hubbert, M. (1956), "Nuclear Energy and the Fossil Fuel", *American Petroleum Institute*, Drilling and Production Practice, 1 January, New York.

Meinert, L., Robinson, G. and Nassar, N. (2016), "Mineral resources: reserves, peak production and the future", *US Geological Survey*, Reston (Virginia).

3 Pollution management

"Al fresco on a beautiful spring day"

ESSENTIAL SUMMARY

A first-order principle derived from Newtonian thermodynamics – the notion that matter can never be destroyed – explains why all inputs found at the beginning of a physical transformation process are also present at its end, albeit in a changed form. A second principle – that all action provokes a reaction – is key to studies of the noxious impact that many companies' activities have on the natural environment. These two scientific effects (attesting to the very real impacts of companies' physical operations) are what make pollution such a key topic in green business studies.

Section I. The pollution framework

Like any corporate behaviour, pollution occurs within a social, political but also scientific context. A useful way of apprehending this is by taking each major pollution category separately and identifying the historical and other factors, in relation to business activities.

Air quality and climate change

Air quality has long been a focal point for environmental critics of the industrial age. As far back as Victorian times, observers lamented the damage being done to forests surrounding the mill towns spread across England's Midlands. This inauspicious beginning was followed a century later by numerous episodes of killer smog, one example being the lethal mixture of fog and coal smoke that killed thousands of Londoners in 1952. Since then, it has been illegal to light a coal fire within Greater London. Entrepreneurs reacted to this new regulation by creating smokeless wood for households to burn. Pollution control has always been viewed by some as a business opportunity (Figure 3.1).

In general, the economic growth that the world's older industrialised countries experienced during the decades following the Second World War translated into skyrocketing industrial manufacturing and above all automobile use – leading in turn to widespread air quality problems in cities all across the Global North. By the 1970s, for instance, things had become so bad in Los Angeles that athletes in this automobile-mad city were regularly forced to abandon daytime activities because the air was dangerous to breathe. As discussed previously, however, the succession of environmental disasters that accumulated during this period sparked new political awareness so that within a few short years, local and national governments in many industrialised nations began enacting anti-pollution measures like vehicle emission standards. This culminated in headline events such as the stringent fuel consumption regulations that Japan adopted in 1999, the European Union's ban on all leaded gasoline on 1 January 2000 or indeed California's 2030 zero-emission vehicle programme. Automakers have been induced and/or forced by tighter controls to lower emissions, leading to platinum-based catalytic converters being affixed on all cars and ultimately to today's wave of fuel-efficient hybrid or electric vehicles. Similar measures have been implemented in relation to other air pollution sources, starting with industrial chimneys. Now, at the dawn of a new millennium, most of the Global North has created a legal framework that theoretically enables progress in the battle against localised smog.

Type	Sources include:
Solid particles	
- Asbestos fibres, dust	Mineral extraction, cement works, steel works, glassworks, quarries
Chemical gases	
- SO_2 Sulphur dioxide	Power stations, refineries, combustion plants
- NOx Nitrogen oxides	International combustion engines, forest fires
- CO Carbon monoxide	Motor vehicle exhaust fumes
- CO_2 Carbon dioxide	Fossil fuels
- VOC volatile organic compounds	Chemical solvents, paints, printing, glues
- CH_4 Methane	Coal mine, landfill sites, livestock
- CFC Chlorofluorocarbons	Aerosol propellants, foams, fire extinguishers, refrigerators
- HF Hydrofluoric acid	Aluminium fusion, glass fibre makers, brickworks
Heavy metals	
- As Arsenic	Glass-making, metal working
- Cd Cadmium	Burning solid mineral fuels, heavy fuel oil
- Cr Chromium	Production of glass, cement, ferrous metals
- Hg Mercury	Chlorine production, waste incineration
- Pb Lead	Fusion of lead, manufacture of batteries
- Se Selenium	Glass production, use of heavy fuel oil
- Zi Zinc	Combustion coal/fuel oil, industrial metals processes, waste incineration
Other pollutants	
- NH_3 Ammonia	Agricultural activities
- PCDD-F Dioxins	Incineration, fuel combusion

Figure 3.1 List of Main Atmospheric Pollutants.

The same cannot be said about many cities in emerging economies, where development has often been seen as a more pressing priority than the ecological imperative. This paradigm is best encapsulated in a construct referred to as the Kuznets curve, or the idea that economic development first causes environmental deterioration before a country achieves the post-industrial standard of living beyond which it starts to prioritise pollution abatement. The problem here is aggravated by the Global South's growing share of world manufacturing, often explained by the lower costs characterising these economies due to their lower wages but also because they tend to have less demanding environmental standards. This reflects a process that international business practitioners refer to as the "race to the bottom", one where impoverished national governments desperate for capital are pressured by multinational enterprises (MNEs) to relax expensive pollution standards or risk seeing the company shop regimes and invest elsewhere. Add to this the poverty of farmers living in the Amazonian or Indonesian rain forests – which is then burnt to create more arable land – and it becomes clear why the prioritisation accorded to the battle against air pollution is often affected by a number of extra-environmental factors.

Heat

A related but even greater challenge has arisen in recent years, namely climate change, an issue that is universal by its very nature. A clear overlap exists between traditional air pollution and this new problem. Whereas some of the particulates spewed into the air since the beginning of the industrial age may reach the atmosphere's lower strata before falling back to the Earth's surface in the form of acid rain, other industrial emissions have released carbon dioxide and other gases into the upper atmosphere, creating what is known as the greenhouse effect. The ensuing risk of potentially uncontrollable global warming is so frightening that no society (or company) in the world can afford to ignore it.

Carbon dioxide calculations are a good starting point for broaching this topic. Before the Industrial Revolution, carbon dioxide levels varied from 180 parts per million (ppm) at times when Earth was cold to 280 ppm during hot periods. After 250 years of industrialisation, it was estimated in the year 2019 that carbon dioxide levels had already hit 414.7 ppm and were rising rapidly. The problem is that to have any real chance of limiting global warming to an average two-degree rise by the year 2030, scientific consensus has been that total emissions must be capped at 450 ppm. In the absence of unimaginably large-scale geo-engineering sequestering existing greenhouse gases, this seems impossible today (Figure 3.2).

	2020	2030	2040	2050
At current rate of annual emission, the number of gigatonnes (GGT) of CO_2 equivalent gas is	55	61	72	85
To keep concentrations down to 550 ppm, annual GGT of CO_2 equivalent emissions must be	47	40	38	32
To keep concentrations down to 450 ppm, annual GGT of CO_2 equivalent emissions must be	31	18	15	14

Figure 3.2 2006 Stern Report CO_2-Level Scenarios.

Rising global temperatures are already causing enormous economic problems. Many crop yields have suffered from the heat, droughts have proliferated, melting polar caps have raised sea levels and intensified coastal flooding, etc. Each of these phenomena has met a business response – respectively, a migration of farmland to zones that were once too cold to cultivate; a whole industry revolving around water conservation technology; a new industry in urban barrier systems, etc. But it would be very wrong to view business created in response to climate change as a net positive. Not only is it impossible to see how companies can thrive in a world where human survival is at risk but even from a narrower perspective, climate change is having terrible effects on many corporate bottom lines – exemplified by the crisis affecting the global insurance industry, hit by the huge losses caused by the greater frequency and intensity of global warming-associated storms. By making meteorological events more erratic, radical climate change also makes it harder for businesses to engage in long-term planning – an instability that then weighs upon managers' investment decisions.

Terrestrial and aquatic damage

Land and water pollution are separate concerns that can be studied as such. Still, it is worth scrutinising the links between the two. On the one hand, water is the main agent transporting pollutants whose sediments often leave toxic deposits in the surrounding soil systems even after the liquid has evaporated. On the other, pollutants stored non-hermetically on land can seep underground and infiltrate aquifers or other water systems. Indeed, the atmospheric pollutants discussed in the previous section also interact continuously with the Earth's terrestrial and aquatic systems. The basic ecological principle of interdependency applies not only at the micro level of chemical reactions but also at the more macro level of the Earth's biosphere.

Terrestrial pollution

Pollutants affect terrestrial environments in different ways. The focus here can be precautionary to assess how different waste forms might best be contained and isolated. Otherwise, analysis can also be sectorial, assessing the soil damage caused by the misuse of agricultural pesticides and fertilisers, the negative externalities associated with many mining practices and the pollution from countless manufacturing, transportation and power generation activities.

The first observation in this respect is that the largest and most hazardous on-land waste streams are rarely perceived by the public eye. Industrial activities generate by far the greatest quantum of pollutants, mainly comprised of so-called non-product output (NPO), a construct recognising that the vast majority of inputs used to make a physical item are not found in the final product itself but consumed during the manufacturing process, at which point they enter the waste stream. This explains why one major industrial greening drive today involves increasing within any given value chain the ratio of products to non-products made using a given quantum of inputs. Note the political difficulty, in a free market economy, for authorities to impose a particular breakdown between intermediary goods and end products. Managers' incentives for altering this ratio mainly depend on cost and technology – but also on their responses to any public outcry caused by negative perceptions of corporate waste practices.

On-land waste management can also be studied in light of many companies' separation of different streams to facilitate future recycling. The idea here is that recyclates' disposal will increasingly be viewed in the future as a profit source rather than a cost centre. Of course, this approach is at odds with a longstanding business strategy called planned obsolescence, where higher quality hence longer-lasting inputs are replaced by cheaper components that generate more hazardous forms of waste when the product in question comes to the end of its working life. The arbitrage between short-term costs and long-term returns is a constant in green business studies.

Lastly, terrestrial pollution cannot be fully analysed without reference to population growth. One over-arching construct in environmental studies (for businesses and individuals alike) is that every human activity has a "footprint", expressed in terms of resources used but also the stresses placed on different ecosystems due to human activity – with pollution in the form of terrestrial waste being a prime "stressor". Since each company (and individual) has a footprint, it stands to reason that notwithstanding efforts made to reduce the magnitude of any singular effects, the greater the number of actors, the greater the overall impact. That being the case, a whole range of analytical sources have publicised their quantification of how many planet Earths are required to sustain human activity on its current scale. Suffice it to say that all have found current living patterns totally unsustainable.

Water pollution

Corporate responsibility for the havoc that pollution has wreaked upon the world's aquatic systems reflects either the widespread misconception that oceanic and other major water bodies are big enough to dilute any volume of pollutants, or else an unwillingness to pay for the clean-up of pollutants for which a business holds its counterparts responsible. Many managers' overriding sense is that water is a common resource, hence an asset for which the state alone has responsibility. The problem is complicated by the fact that bodies of water do not recognise national borders, with pollution originating in one jurisdiction easily ending up in another. This means that national governments will have a similar interest in not paying for clean-ups because they do not want neighbouring governments to get a "free ride" at their expensive. In the absence of global governance mechanisms supported by members willing to pool anti-pollution costs, it is difficult to see how this incentive for inaction (or disincentive to act) might be resolved.

On other occasions, even when a company has been identified by a government body as being guilty of egregious water pollution, the state may not always prosecute to the full extent of the law. Such inaction is often explained away by an administration lacking the resources to bring cases of misconduct to court, or else by an ideological reluctance to harshly penalise parties deemed to create value for society in other ways. In reality, the crux here is the arbitrage that a society makes between human (and planetary) health versus private business interests – judgements that tend to vary depending on a host of factors, including the scale and frequency of the polluting activities as well as the perceived importance of the company's activities.

Section II. Corporate pollution behaviour

Alongside these social, political and scientific frameworks, pollution can also be studied at a more micro level reflecting individual businesses' behaviour in this area (and accounting thereof). After all, pollution is not just a topic of prime importance to society, it has also become increasingly important in determining companies' brand reputation, employee motivation and incentive to innovate – not to mention legal liabilities.

Activity-based analysis

Green business understanding in this area often starts by comparing point, line and surface sources of pollution. The first category refers to emissions, effluents and other outflows with a single identifiable origin that can be either movable or stationary. Line pollution refers the sum total of the waste coming from a particular activity, without any distinction as to the source. Surface source pollution refers to contaminated effluents running off urban or rural surfaces. Note that a further distinction can be made between pollutants' area of impact (upper atmosphere, the Earth's surface, deep underground or some combination thereof) and whether they occur constantly or intermittently.

The reason why it is so important to distinguish pollution categories is because each requires a different set of responses. Depending on whether a particular category has a single identifiable origin or if it affects one or many actors, there will be a marked variation in companies' liability. A socially valued activity with a small negative impact on one single actor will provoke a very different response than a less valued activity devastating an entire community. Pollution is a broad term encompassing different situations. A business will therefore apprehend it in a variety of ways.

Usually, the main focus will involve examining the damage caused when pollutants interact with their surroundings, i.e. the level of toxicity. This will depend on a host of factors, starting with "dilution" or the principle that the lower the concentration of a pollutant in proportion to the agents (water, solvents) capable of dissipating its effects, the greater the chance of containing any negative externalities. Thus, an element that is non-toxic in small doses can become toxic in larger quantities. Of course, the notion of concentration must be understood in this context not only in volume and quantity terms but also as regards the pollutant's capacity for causing harm (and the ease with which it can be disarmed). Clearly, radioactive waste from a nuclear power station causes greater harm and dilutes less effectively (or indeed, not at all) than de-greased sludge taken from factory machines. Problems of this nature have sparked enormous business interest in the field of green chemistry.

Other analyses focus more on how pollutants disperse from their point(s) of origin. Liquids, solids and gases spread throughout the environment at varying speeds. In turn, this affects surrounding ecosystems' ability to withstand their presence. In general, solids are the preferred form of waste disposal since it is comparatively easier to contain their seepage into the surrounding environment. Indeed, some companies' pollution strategies start with the transformation of liquids or gases into solids – a prime example being when industrialists insert scrubbers inside their factory chimneys to capture particles that would otherwise be spewed out as gas. Of course, such "end-of-pipeline" systems are expensive, raising questions as to the company's willingness (or obligation) to assume the costs of pollution control.

Otherwise and as aforementioned, the clear and present danger of global warming has turned gaseous emissions into a paramount concern for many businesses nowadays. The complication here is identifying the origins of such emissions, whose dispersion depends on many variables. Micro-environments everywhere are prone to different pollution patterns, meaning that the same emission can have different effects in different locations. This has direct implications for the kind of immediate pressures that the companies responsible for such emissions are likely to face.

The same can be said about pollutants in liquid form, even though the origins of these releases are sometimes easier to identify, hence sanction. A large corpus of research exists on the effects of liquid effluents, often focusing on their level of noxiousness and speed of dispersion. Such determinations highlight the key role that scientists play in debates about levels of toxicity that a given environment is resilient enough to withstand. Much analysis in this area includes discussion about the thresholds beyond which pollution's damaging effects can no longer be contained. One problem arising from this is that business (and more broadly, public) recognition of the urgency of addressing a given pollution problem is often out of date, i.e. by the time managers are ready and willing to implement a certain level of anti-pollution measures, the problem has already worsened to the point of requiring further remedy.

Other ways in which companies account for the pollution they produce include the geographic area affected and the duration of toxicity. The only way to ensure a complete inventory of corporate pollutants would be for all companies worldwide to engage in a full and honest accounting of their total physical inputs and outputs. This kind of reporting is starting to take root but remains very patchy, with different countries, sectors and/or companies displaying varying degrees of willingness to assume the costs associated with full-blown environmental accounting. It is also difficult for companies making products using components sourced worldwide to have a clear picture of the environmental footprint of the "embedded inputs" within the supplies they procure. Business pollution analysis is generally plagued by an absence of comprehensive data.

Sector analysis

The physicality of primary and secondary sector activities means that they are the direct cause of most corporate pollution. Note that this book does not share some analysts' vision of a de-materialised tertiary sector. After all, service sector companies are still operating in a physical world. It is simply easier to analyse their footprint within the confines of the primary and secondary sector activities supporting their efforts.

There is a lack of data about the sectorial breakdown of corporate pollution except in the one area dominating many analysts' attention today – greenhouse gases. Here, the general understanding is that from 35 to 40 percent of global carbon dioxide emissions comes from industrial sources (led by a few main sectors such as cement, petroleum refining and metallurgy); 30–35 percent from the built environment; and around 25 percent from transportation. These numbers vary markedly from one country to another, however, reflecting factors such as climate variations, different uses of passenger cars versus public transportation, the availability of factory-level anti-pollution technology or national natural resource endowments. In all likelihood, concentrating anti-pollution efforts in a few key sectors could produce disproportionate environmental benefits. Conversely, it may be less efficient for a society, operating at a macro level, to make investments in this way. The problem, of course, is that societies do not take macro decisions of this kind – it is companies operating at a micro level who do.

Primary activities

The main pollution problem with agriculture is soil quality, a constraint that countless farmers have faced since the dawn of time. In simple terms, the soil covering the face of the Earth is itself a biotic organism comprised not only of "dead" rocks but also living nutrients sustained by organic matter. These nutrients are also the agents providing plants with the sustenance they need to grow. Once plants die, they decompose into further nutrients (sometimes called "humus") that will feed later generations, thereby creating a sustainable fertility cycle. Problems arise if something perturbs the process.

Ironically, the very agents that farmers use to maximise crop yields, pesticides, have long been criticised for the toxic residues that they leave behind (and which are all the more dangerous since they can ultimately accumulate in human tissue). As for nitrogen-based fertilisers, these have also become very inefficient, with as little as 30 percent of the quantities being disseminated actually interacting with plant life. The rest tends to run off from fields and accumulate in global water systems (onshore and subsequently offshore), causing de-oxygenated dead zones in which sea life cannot live. Note additionally the long-term impoverishment of soil when too much fertiliser has been used – a prime example being the problems experienced in the once fertile southern reaches of California's Central Valley.

The other primary activity with serious pollution problems is mining. One common practice involves using toxic chemicals such as arsenic to separate minerals from dirt, without proper disposal of the ensuing slurry. Another "enviro-crime" is the habit of using explosives to scalp off entire mountaintops simply because this makes it easier for mining companies to access underground ore – with the subsequent debris being dumped randomly and killing off entire ecosystems. Lastly, the leakage of heavy metals from decommissioned mines is often a major source of groundwater pollution. Most interesting here is that these effects only become visible years after a mine has been abandoned. Many companies' pollution behaviour in this like other areas of activity can only be accurately assessed years later, once all residual consequences of today's actions have had time to manifest.

Secondary activities

It is impossible to list all the different ways in which manufacturing activities cause pollution. Nevertheless, there is value in noting two seminal principles in this area.

- Industrial products are the summation of a multitude of processes and value chains, each of which has its own footprint. The pollution associated with them should therefore not be analysed in singular terms but as a cumulative total.

- Modern industry's relatively infrequent use of biodegradable inputs means that more and more goods are made out of materials whose life spans are much longer than the functional purposes for which they were originally designed. Examples range from the e-waste caused by the mountains of outdated electronic equipment accumulating on dumpsites worldwide; to most if not all forms of plastic packaging plaguing today's terrestrial and aquatic environments. As these synthetic products degrade, they often release uncontrolled toxic substances into the environment.

In terms of specific activities, the greatest quantum of pollution derives from the power generation sector, although there is a debate here whether utility companies or their customers should ultimately be held responsible. The pollution generated during the production and distribution of electricity, for instance, depends on a host of factors, including which primary fuel is consumed to generate the current. Note as well that this is the sector where the greatest improvements stand to be achieved, depending on the speed with which so-called dirty energy sources are replaced by cleaner variants (i.e. renewables). The optimistic lesson here is that those sectors that create the most pollution are also the ones where there may be the greatest value (hence business interest) in developing remedies.

Lastly, transportation activities are often portrayed as the second leading cause of industrial pollution. This is due to the huge size of the global market for passenger vehicles, almost all of which have been powered until now by smog-producing, petrol-based internal combustion engines. On top of this, there is the more structural problem of MNEs outsourcing logistics activities following the globalisation of many modern supply chains. The problem is that some MNEs overlook the quality of the third-party logistics services they commission – creating a grey area of accountability that can often lead to non-quality and environmental disaster. Examples include recurring instances of terrible oil spills caused by cheap transporters' use of sub-standard vehicles. In the end, the battle against corporate pollution is as much a question of managerial prioritisation as an issue of scientific knowledge.

Bibliography

Berners-Lee, M. (2010), *How Bad Are Bananas? The Carbon Footprint of Everything*, Green Profile, London.

Kuznets, S. (1955), "Economic growth and income inequality", *American Economic Review*, Volume 45, pp. 1–28.

Markham, A. (1994), *A Brief History of Pollution*, Earthscan, London.

Rockstrom, J. et al. (2009), *Planetary Boundaries: Exploring the Safe Operating Space for Humanity*, Portland State University Institute for Sustainable Solutions Publications, Oregon.

World Health Organisation Air Pollution website: https://www.who.int/airpollution/en/

4 Environmental economics and policies

"Eating himself into an early grave"

ESSENTIAL SUMMARY

Green business refers to the physical and scientific realities studied in the two previous chapters – as well as the paradigms applied by the decision-makers creating the economic and political frameworks within which this new management approach materialises. The first step is to identify differences between environmental economics and classical economics, such as the latter have been understood and applied for several centuries now. It then becomes useful to ascertain to what extent these economic sensitivities have translated into concrete policies and regulations affecting businesspersons' ability to act in this new field. This is crucial because in the environmental realm like so many others, economics and politics tend to evolve hand-in-hand.

Section I. Environmental economics

There is little doubt that market-oriented economics have dominated the international business landscape since the early 1980s, taking over from earlier paradigms that tended to be more accepting of state "interventionism". Attitudes will of course continue to evolve in the future – economic paradigms are largely cyclical, with shifts usually occurring when a crisis causes disenchantment with the status quo. One initial debate in the field of environmental economics is whether societies perceive Planet Earth's current ecological situation as a crisis, and if so, the chances that this will engender a new global paradigm.

Incompatibilities between classical and environmental economics

In 1776, Adam Smith wrote the seminal treatise that laid the foundations for modern capitalism, asserting that individuals should have the freedom to conduct their economic affairs as they see fit. This reflected in part Smith's assessment that individuals will normally seek to maximise their material self-interest, with the sum total of their efforts combining to maximise global welfare. Market pricing is key to this process, signalling to buyers or sellers whether they should change their demand or supply behaviour, culminating over the long run in an equilibrium that ensures an optimal allocation of resources is reached.

Smith's economics have been debated throughout history, perhaps most cogently in the 1936 writings of the British economist John Maynard Keynes. Noting that "in the long term, we are all dead", Keynes demonstrated the dangers of developing economic theory solely based on market mechanisms while ignoring the social costs associated with any re-allocation of resources. This is not to say that classical economics lack merit or that Smith's premise of human self-interest is invalid. Indeed, ample evidence exists to suggest that market mechanisms can be a relatively efficient way of organising many economic interactions. However, as is the case with all general theories, there are flaws in Smith's construct, with at least two assumptions – that amalgamated self-interest translates into optimal group outcomes and that price is an accurate signal of value – making his economics at least partially incompatible with environmental realities.

Self-interest vs. group interest

In 1968, University of California at Santa Barbara Professor Garrett Hardin wrote a seminal text in modern environmental economics, postulating a "tragedy of the commons" situation in which individual shepherds discover open meadows where their herds can graze for free, something each understandably wants to do. The problem lies in the biological reality of meadows like any other ecosystem. If sheep consume grass more slowly than it replenishes biologically, then their pursuit of self-interest remains sustainable and they can continue indefinitely. However, once other shepherds join or the number of sheep rises to the point of eating the grass all the way to its roots – exceeding its replenishment threshold – the meadow will die, meaning that the advantage will disappear. In other words, in a biological world, it is the very act of maximising short-term self-interest that destroys long-term self-interest – an effect that does not figure in Smith's economics.

One implication of Hardin's construct is that rival economic actors will necessarily dilapidate public goods in the absence of an authority regulating access. The question then becomes whether public or private sector parties should allocate use of a common resource and police its access. One opinion at this level came from economist Elinor Ostrom, awarded the Nobel Prize for demonstrating that individuals in a commons situation are capable of banding together to form collectives capable of assuming organisational responsibilities. In any event, the tragedy of the commons is a strong construct highlighting some of classical economics' limitations in conditions defined by real ecological constraints.

Mispricing and disincentives

Hawkens and Lovins' construct of "natural capitalism" – referring to the endemic under-pricing of vulnerable and/or finite natural resources – is another area where classical economics do not account for ecological realities. The premise here is that capitalism in its current form only functions because the natural world (and/or future generations) pay subsidies enabling current generations to live beyond their means. In classical theory, if the supply of a commodity falls behind the demand, the price will rise, in which case demand is destined to fall. The problem is that this basic mechanism does not work very well when demand for finite resources is inelastic due to a lack of substitutes. A second more micro-level problem is that companies who do price a natural resource at its real value might find it difficult to pass this on to customers, with higher costs at the early upstream stage of a global value chain either being subtracted from manufacturers' profits or inflating end users' purchasing price. As for supply-side behaviour, according to classical theory, rising prices should motivate producers to increase output and/or innovate. Yet this is by definition constrained in situations where supplies are finite and where change is disincentivised by erratic price signals, institutional inertia and/or sunk investments.

To complicate matters, economic actors often feign not to be able to read the pricing signals emitted by today's overuse and/or misuse of natural resources. Most managers are very aware of the environmental bind in which the world find itself but still hide behind the excuse that some unnamed party will come up with a magic solution remedying these problems. Yet others may calculate, quite cynically, that impending ecological disasters will only arise at some unspecified point in the future, once they have maximised their personal gains from today's unsustainable economics. They may justify this to themselves after witnessing the penalty paid by those actors who had the foresight to invest in green business but got in too early. Many environmental technologies and products remain at their infant stage or else have not attained the critical mass that will allow them to achieve economies of scale and attract new buyers, thereby triggering the kind of virtuous circle that helps new business to take off. Classical economics argue that markets should be allowed to achieve equilibrium in their own time. Environmental economics, on the other hand, argues that after years of burdening Earth's ecosystems, such patience is an unaffordable luxury. The two disciplines work to entirely different timescales.

Difficulties formulating a new discipline

A cogent body of theory cannot be solely based on criticisms of its predecessors but must also contain its own coherence. Some good work has therefore been achieved developing theories specific to "ecological economics", a more narrowly focused sub-discipline than "environmental economics". The key idea here is that economic development must be understood in qualitative rather than quantitative terms. Note that this conception – rejection of growth for growth's sake – has become more mainstream in recent years and spread far beyond the environmental movement, with increasing numbers of world leaders starting to question if gross domestic product (GDP) growth is a suitable indicator of well-being.

A second seminal principle sets ecological economics in a context defined by natural sciences. Here, leading figures like Romanian mathematician Nicholas Georgescu-Roegen have built first-order theories around Newton's laws of thermodynamics, postulating that the dispersion of energy witnessed in nature (so-called entropy) is also an economic reality. The premise here is that true efficiency means maximising the amount of energy (derived directly or indirectly from the sun) that can be used for economic purposes and indeed recycled to become new inputs for future activities. Conversely, to the extent that resource depletion (the over-exploitation of "natural capital") and/or pollution undermine the Earth's "carrying capacity" or ability to sustain life, all human activity is bound to suffer from diminishing returns until such time as sufficient technological progress has been achieved to rectify this disfunction.

Ecological economics also maintains that it is wrong to assert, as classical economists do, that assets' future value should necessarily be discounted to reflect their present value. Quite the contrary, capitalising an asset's present value into the future by extending its useful lifespan via resource and/or energy conservation is deemed a superior measure of economic efficiency. This is a very aspirational sub-branch of economics, one whose application is quite problematic given widespread belief in many if not most societies that success can only be measured in monetary terms. For most businesses, the chief priority is maximising shareholder value. Some of the values conveyed through ecological economics are at odds with this mindset.

Because environmental economics do incorporate monetary perspectives, they tend to receive a wider airing than their ecological sibling. Yet neither of these sub-disciplines enjoys as serious a reputation as many other branches of economics. This may be because neither has fully resolved two fundamental questions in this field: how to assess value; and how to attribute responsibility. Once theorisation advances in these areas, environmental and ecological economics are likely to become more mainstream.

Difficult assessment of ecological value

In line with the environmentalist premise that physical (and social) interactions can only be assessed accurately in light of the diverse range of interdependencies that sustain life, ecological value depends on a whole host of parameters. These include culture-based views of the natural world; attitudes regarding materialism in general; experiences of habitat stewardship; and the general availability of natural resources at a given moment in history. A well-known construct called "Maslow's hierarchy" argues cogently, for instance, that actors will only prioritise certain goals once basic material needs such as food and shelter have been satisfied. This underpins an ongoing international business debate about the extent to which environmentalism should be deemed an absolute priority in the world's poorer nations.

The assessment of ecological value is further complicated by other factors as well. At one level, it is extremely difficult to calculate what resources should be spent on biodiversity to enable the survival of species that produce no material economic value per se but contribute to the health of an overall ecosystem. At another, it is almost impossible to ascertain the monetary value of investing today to ensure that unborn future generations will enjoy a healthy and bio-diverse ecosphere. Value assessments based on the arbitrage between the present and the future can be found in all economic disciplines but certain subjectivities in the field of environmental economics make the calculation even harder here.

Similar problems arise when ascertaining the respective value of competing demands for resources. This can be exemplified by the arbitrage between human material wealth and the rights of flora and fauna. In the past, only very marginal and/or utopian movements would advocate giving rights to non-humans. However, recent bodies of law that restrict cruelty to animals have set a more mainstream precedent for this credo. Any figures quantified in this area are bound, however, to be highly arbitrary.

Lastly, ecological problems do not have the same effect on all constituencies in a given society at a given point in time. Some populations live in proximity to beautiful pristine environments – others (usually less privileged ones) near polluted wastelands. The concept of ecological justice means that situations should also be valued according to the extent to which each affects and/or is caused by a narrow or broad cross-section of society. Fairness and community solidarity are issues in environmental economics, perhaps even more than in neighbouring branches.

Attribution of responsibility

One widespread criticism of classical economics – perhaps the most severe – is that it does not account for the reality of market failure, or situations where normal market mechanisms have resulted in a suboptimal allocation of resources. Conversely, market failure is widely assumed in environmental economics, one of whose seminal constructs is the existence of negative externalities, a leading example of which is when the pollution caused by one party's activity (i.e. factories) causes harm (i.e. bad air quality) to innocent bystanders who did nothing to deserve this disadvantage. Externalities of this kind are economically inefficient since they let "free rider" actors get away with not paying for the damage they have caused. By definition, this means an irrational allocation of value – the epitome of poor economics (Figure 4.1).

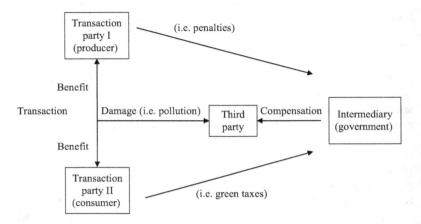

Figure 4.1 Redistribution (Dis)advantages After a Negative Environmental Externality.

With a negative externality such as pollution, it is almost impossible for the market alone to devise an appropriate price structure, due to the absence of any direct relationship between the party causing the damage and the party suffering from it. Ensuring a compensatory redistribution of value requires intermediation, which outside of the marketplace is likely to be either the state (via the tax system) or else a competent body which has been delegated authority towards this end – increasingly nowadays on a cross-border level.

The traditional principle that environmental economics applies in relation to this problem is to ensure that the "polluter pays", with penalties assessed so that the party responsible for the externality pays its cost (i.e. "internalises" it). The hope here is that the perpetrator will be dissuaded from repeating the harmful behaviour and, in this particular case, invest in new systems generating less pollution. The economic difficulty lies in calculating how high the penalties must be to incentivise better behaviour. Clearly, the higher the penalties, the greater the probability that the polluter will change. Historically, however, business lobbies have been effective at convincing governments not to impose "punitive" levies – the net effect of which is to often make it more economic for polluters to pay a fine but continue to pollute.

Note along these lines the greater cost of "mitigating" pollution (not producing it in the first place) as opposed to "abatement" (cleaning up afterwards). Given the levels of pollutants that have already accumulated in the ecosphere, mere abatement is seldom enough to achieve ecological restoration. It is, however, very prevalent, if only because actors can then claim that they are facing up to their environmental responsibilities without this costing them too much. One example is the practice of carbon offsetting, exemplified by the Clean Development Mechanism (CDM) that came out of the 1997 Kyoto Protocol on Climate Change. CDM does not ask wealthy countries to fulfil their greenhouse gas reduction goals by cutting their own emissions but instead lets them simply fund new clean energy projects in the Global South. A similar criticism of the "cap and trade" trading schemes currently being rolled out in many countries to address the climate change crisis is that carbon dioxide permit allocations are too high to motivate real change – especially since polluters exceeding their allocations can simply buy other participants' unused allowances. Ecologically, these schemes would be more effective if governments simply prohibited anyone from exceeding their assigned limits. In a democratic market economy, however, such authoritarianism seems fairly inconceivable. In the environmental arena like many others, there is an indelible link between economics and politics.

Section II. Environmental policy

There will always be a debate between those who trust companies to develop green business without government intervention and others who doubt that market mechanisms alone can achieve this. Many environmentalists have expressed disappointment with a general lack of progress in the new century. The take-up of energy-efficient products has been patchy; investment in renewable energy is slow; and global manufacturing's ecological footprint is as unsustainable as ever. To a certain extent, the reluctance with which most sectors are adopting fully green business practices is a manifestation of market failure. Hence environmentalists' frequent call nowadays for greater state involvement materialised through policy.

Global policy frameworks

Environmental policy frameworks determine a whole range of corporate rights, opportunities and obligations. Even if certain advanced nations tend to set the pace, enormous global variations in enactment and implementation make it almost impossible for any one company to keep informed of all relevant legislation and policy in this field – explaining why environmental consultancy has in recent years become one of many markets' fastest growing service activity.

Notwithstanding the risk of regime arbitrage – where companies specifically move operations to benefit from lax hence inexpensive standards – many environmental policy decisions remain specific to particular contexts. The ensuing lack of cross-border harmonisation explains the widespread belief that environmental policy can only be effectively pursued if agreed at a global level. This is especially true given the hierarchical superiority of international agreements – once they have been ratified – over national and local laws. The same idea can also be expressed in pure business terms, namely that the intensification of trade argues for a concomitant internationalisation of environmental policy.

The UN, as the closest thing to a world government, has quite naturally taken a lead in this respect, organising over the years many high-profile conferences that have helped to drive environmental concerns further up member-states' agenda. The problem for the UN is that its conferences have often been criticised as talking shops lacking the power to enforce the policies they decide. The question then becomes which intergovernmental organisation might fulfil this policing role – a real challenge since the only other body with the scope to potentially assume responsibility for environmental policy, namely the World Trade Organisation (WTO), has declined to add this competency to its area of jurisdiction. Moreover, even if a "World Environmental Organisation" were to be created, it would have a very difficult task. First, assessing global environmental performance is very challenging given the enormous variation in countries' monitoring abilities. Second, no global consensus exists regarding what level of penalties should be applied to environmental misconduct. Lastly, it is unclear how to allocate responsibility for cross-border environmental damage whose origins are uncertain – especially given the strong free rider incentive in this situation to try to get partner nations to foot the bill.

All of these problems relate to the definition of jurisdictions, or the extent to which one state has the right to decide – possibly without consent – that it can and should oversee behaviour affecting the common good but occurring outside of its borders. In a few cases, a cross-border environmental oversight function of this kind will fit seamlessly into an existing regional arrangement. Most of the time, however, territoriality creates real dilemmas that – unless a political and legal resolution can be found – prevent governments with strong environmental credentials from policing companies operating within the borders of less environmentally demanding neighbours. The latter can then become "pollution havens", inducing less scrupulous multinational enterprises (MNEs) to engage in "environmental dumping" strategies where their production location decisions are largely driven by a desire to escape stringent environmental oversight. Hence, one school of thought that the only global bodies truly capable of assuming responsibility for the implementation of global environmental policy are MNEs themselves.

This is not a straightforward proposition, since private sector MNEs' fiduciary responsibility to shareholders means they are under constant pressure to increase margins, resulting under certain conditions in suboptimal environmental performance. Having said that, MNEs left to their devices will often locate production activities in countries whose comparative advantage augments overall productivity – thereby reducing waste, the very epitome of a sustainable business practice.

National policy instruments

At the narrower level of national governance, green policy-making depends on a whole slew of factors. One is a society's subjective consensus as to how much of a priority the environment has become, hence how much pressure should be put on government to intervene. The problem is that above and beyond media campaigns waged by activist environmentalist groups like Greenpeace or the World Wildlife Fund, it can be difficult to gauge the electorate's attitude towards specific green issues. A recent example is how majority opinions have evolved (sometimes within one and the same constituency) regarding headline issues like off-shore drilling or nuclear power. Even among those citizens who recognise an urgent need for environmental action, there can be wide variations in attitudes towards the legitimacy of state action: whether this should be done on a systematic or ad hoc basis; and above all, whether public monies should be directly earmarked for environmental expenditures or instead if it suffices that business be given incentives to act.

In relation to the former aspect – often materialising in what a number of governments have called their "green new deal" – it is worth exploring to what extent a correlation exists between political parties' attitudes towards statist policies and their willingness to invest directly in green business. Sometimes it is the electorate's perception of the existence of an environmental crisis that legitimises a government's green spending decisions. On other occasions, a green stimulus package might be viewed as a general remedy to an economic recession – even as other voices view such expenditures as wasteful. The legitimacy of direct government spending on environmental issues crosses over into many ostensibly unrelated areas of political philosophy.

Otherwise and as regards the indirect green (dis)incentives that governments can create, it is worth noting that some policies (like official greenhouse gas emission reduction targets) can only be achieved if consumers (through higher purchasing prices) or businesses (through lower margins) spend money on them. This means that the targeted environmental gain will also translate into a fall in certain parties' disposable income. Conversely, other green policies (like a reduction in import tariffs levied on energy-efficient equipment) will ultimately have a beneficial pecuniary effect by reducing costs for those parties that avail themselves of the new opportunities. As such, a more balanced way of analysing the full range of national environmental policies (see Figure 4.2) is that they will produce a variety of effects – and

Policy	Details
Public interest criteria	Determination of the conditions under which a government might justify intervention for environmental reasons
Corporate liability	Definition of potential environmental accountability and scope for redress
License to operate	Permission to open a business might be withheld if it fails to demonstrate acceptable environment performance
Elimination of tariffs on green goods and services	Facilitating cross-border trade in green technologies by minimising protectionist restrictions on imports
Carbon trading schemes (cap and trade)	Auction mechanism launched after government determines sector allocations and decides whether to charge for permits and/or set an initial carbon price
Standards	Governments set quantitative targets (emissions, fuel efficiency, etc.) and levy sanctions if they are missed
State-sponsored R&D	Due to the expense and long payback period associated with green innovation, governments often provide financial, infrastructure and/or scientific assistance
Green taxes	Incentivise consumers to opt for greener products (cars, appliances) and/or behaviour (fuel taxes, airport taxes)
Green subsidies	Payments allowing operators to offer green products/services that are competitive at current market prices. Often monitored by international body (WTO, EU) to prevent unfair advantage. Putative entrepreneurs can be offered tax to spark inwards investment
Direct state investment	Government-owned and managed enterprises specialising in the creation/operation of a green business

Figure 4.2 Main Green Policy Tools Used by State Entities.

that it is likely that those parties who align themselves with the new circumstances will perform better than those who simply pay for it. The uncertainties characterising this rapidly evolving area of activity explain MNEs' growing demand for public affairs professionals with a specialisation in environmental policy.

Bibliography

Barbier, E. (2010), *A Global Green New Deal*, Cambridge University Press, Cambridge (UK).

Doppelt, B. (2012), *From Me to We: The Five Transformational Commitments Required to Rescue the Planet, Your Organization, and Your Life*, Greenleaf, Sheffield (UK).

Harden, G. (1968), "The tragedy of the commons", *Science*, Volume 162, Issue 3859, pp. 1243–1248.

Hawken, P. et al. (2005), *Natural Capitalism: The Next Industrial Revolution*, Routledge, USA.

Ostrom, E. (2009), "A general framework for analyzing sustainability of social-ecological systems", *Science*, Volume 325, Issue 5939, pp. 419–422.

5 Going green: managing the process

"Take a seat. You can build it yourself"

ESSENTIAL SUMMARY

For many companies, the transition to green business practices fits into a general corporate social responsibility (CSR) agenda. Theorists have long debated the role that business should play in attending to broader social and environmental problems. A key aspect of this debate is the effect on corporate earnings. Whatever wider benefits sustainability has, bottom-line considerations will always be paramount in business.

Section I. Impetus to go green

The best way of categorising the drive behind any corporate greening process is to determine whether the main goal is "playing to win" (increasing earnings through lower costs, higher revenues and/or improved brand image); "playing not to lose" (avoiding higher costs or potential liabilities); or combining the two and redefining the company's mission statement in this way. To some extent, strategic intent is revealed in the way that the new green activities are accounted for. Where outlays are booked as extraordinary, one-off project costs, there is a strong hint that the entire effort is aimed at minimising environment-related problems; but if they are categorised as capital expenditures, it could be better to conceive of them as a more positive statement of intent.

A second distinction can then be made between top-down green initiatives initiated by senior executives versus more bottom-up approaches driven by frontline change agents. Each has its own peculiarities in terms of speed of implementation, level of commitment and staging. Executive-driven strategies tend to be more procedural in nature, bottom-up initiatives more ad hoc. A number of companies have hybridised the two.

Top-down greening

Executive commitment is obviously key to the adoption and implementation of a green business strategy – especially in centralised firms controlled by all-powerful headquarters. The approach is likelier to institutionalise green paradigms and help them permeate the corporate culture. It also obviates the risk that certain parts of a company internalise a new paradigm while other resist and even undermine the effort. This is because senior executives are the only people in a position to ensure that all corporate functions embrace green thinking.

The question then becomes why an executive might suddenly choose to place green business at the core of his/her mission statement. Sometimes, the difficulty of complying with stringent green regulations is seen as a good thing since it forces a company to remodel itself in a way that will ultimately increase competitiveness. On other occasions, however, the impetus is imitation and conformism. If a company's direct competitors or if global corporate icons convert to a more sustainable approach – overtly and with great fanfare – it becomes harder not to follow suit.

Executives' sense for the environment can also vary from one sector to another. One factor is an activity's tendency to use a greater or lesser amount of natural resources as part of its normal business cycle. Another is the company's specific exposure: water quality will be a key concern for beverage companies whereas large supermarkets might focus more on lighting or refrigeration. To create enthusiasm through a few early wins, executives may initially concentrate on "low-hanging fruit", i.e. improvements that can be achieved with a minimum of pain. The risk, however, is that harder projects become seen as less of a priority. The transition to green business will always be challenging – if it were inexpensive and/or easy, more companies would have been done it by now.

As the people responsible for long-term strategic planning, senior executives are ultimately the ones who will be held accountable for their organisation going green, and ensuring that all structures and business systems are aligned with this direction. This brings personal psychological factors into the greening progress, reflecting factors like variable willingness to eschew short-term gratification and invest in the future (relevant to any cost/benefit analysis of green business) or general acceptance of change. There is an innate inertia in management, dictated by past choices made about systems structuring the full range of corporate activities (like accounting protocols). Going green means shaking all of these systems up, a prospect more conservative executives may find daunting. The end result is that one and the same strategic intent will be implemented in different ways in different companies.

Of course, it is one thing for business executives to recognise the need for change but quite another to give midlevel managers the green light to implement it. The risk here is that the corporate greening process never advances beyond sporadic or even token gestures. Executives may define policy but it is frontline operatives who determine if it will succeed or fail.

Employee buy-in

Corporate greening processes occur in contexts shaped by organisations' general culture. One aspect of this is the expectation that policy innovations will originate in global headquarters or instead be decentralised to the subsidiary level. Another is whether the new policy is something that the company's customers are demanding or instead an idea being pushed by its own operatives.

The question then becomes which level within the company has sparked this search for a new modus operandi. In certain business cultures, the drive can come from frontline workers and midlevel managers, realising through their daily activities that there is a need to change and communicating this to executives who might otherwise have been unaware or even disinterested. The alternatives then are whether these early bottom-up signals receive a strong positive response from executives or, in the worst case, if the messengers are treated as irritants. In this latter instance, one possible response is that employees design a bottom-up reorganisation of working practices without seeking prior managerial approval. Such initiatives will usually be limited by participants' budgetary constraints and lack of authority, however, culminating as often as not in confrontation which might go as high as the company's executive committee (or even annual general meeting) before finding resolution. Depicting the environment as a staff health and safety issue can facilitate its acceptance.

An intermediate scenario sees senior management offer one or two relatively superficial responses (a few LED light bulbs, a few recycling bins) to facilitate acceptance of a greening drive. These small improvements may be useful but can also undermine any sense of urgency about addressing the true scale of a company's environmental footprint. Rejoicing in small greening measures may solidify cooperation between staff and senior management but it can also blind participants to the full extent of the effort.

Of course, sometimes employee buy-in is not a question of bottom-up greening but of overcoming operatives' resistance to change that has been suggested by senior management (particularly problematic when a great hierarchical distance exists between corporate levels). The causes for this reticence may be people's reluctance to change longstanding working habits, a general disinterest in sustainability or fears that green business practices make work harder. The key here is creating a greater sense of relevance hence engagement, often by sharing information and information to give employees the feeling that they have a personal stake in the process. After all, frontline operatives are often the people most directly affected by a company's environmental footprint – particularly the pollution it creates.

The question then becomes what is the best way of developing a common mindset welcoming the transition to greener business practices. At one level, it seems likely that in non-authoritarian cultures, chances of effecting change are greater when this is framed not as a regulatory compliance issue but as reflecting employees' self-interest – taking care all the while to ensure that the message is not communicated in a way that might be considered patronising.

Since green innovation can come from anywhere and anyone, companies often make organisational changes to advance the agenda. The basic choice here is between establishing mobile task forces comprised of dedicated "sustainability coordinators" working horizontally to cascade knowledge of best green practices across departments, or else embedding

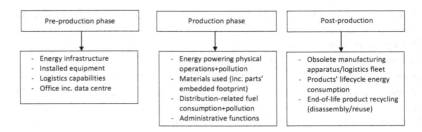

Figure 5.1 You Only Manage What You Measure. Leading Environmental Management System Indicators.

bespoke green specialists in each division. Otherwise, some companies interact with employees in a less structured way, with Human Resource managers working instead to devise personal incentives getting staff on board with the green agenda. This can involve pecuniary rewards such as bonuses based on individual environmental performance. Even more frequent are non-financial rewards such as changes in employees' work/life balance ("flextime" arrangements involving fewer but longer days at the office); public transportation subsidies; employee-organised carpools or cycling initiatives; and, above all, telecommuting ("home-working"), which translates into fewer people being in the office at any one time – enabling the company to downsize its premises even as it reduces its commuting-relating greenhouse gas emissions.

The only constant in modern organisational greening processes is that they involve too many stakeholders to ever be considered linear or one-dimensional. Simply bolting environmentalism onto existing structures may be easier, but it rarely suffices. Change in this area must be systemic and it must be managed – requiring, in the famous words of Peter Drucker, that it be measured (Figure 5.1).

Section II. Controls and measurements

The demarcation between internal metrics used for performance benchmarking purposes and external reporting attesting to company achievements can be somewhat artificial. Indicators devised internally are often publicised externally. Conversely, many corporate auditing metrics were modelled after external guidelines. Whether this involves sectorial initiatives, national legislations or international codes of conduct, the end result is that there can be great variation in the quality of environmental information provided by different companies in different countries.

In general, managers will want to concentrate greening measurements on those environmental indicators that are most relevant to the specific fields where their company operates. It bears repeating that green business strategies are always formulated in specific contexts reflecting the main environmental problems that a given company faces. Attempts to monitor all problems at all times are actually problematic – information overload is as much of a problem in green business as it is in other disciplines. The best green auditing tends to scrutinise a narrowly defined area in great depth rather than treating a wider dataset more superficially.

Internal metrics

There is no single standardised ideal-type model specifying metrics enabling environmental performance measurement up and down the corporate value chain. In some countries, government agencies can provide useful materials; in others, these tend to come from business associations. Alongside of this, companies seeking to qualify for leading reporting groups such as the International Organisation for Standardisation (ISO) or the Global Reporting Initiative (GRI) can get information from these bodies about the green audits they must undertake before and after joining. Many consultancy firms (private and non-profit alike) sell environmental data and impact assessment toolkits and training programme assessments. The real problem here is subsuming the diverse recommendations that companies receive into a specific environmental management system (EMS).

Other problems can arise once the EMS has been designed. This can involve accessing information (i.e. ascertaining the quantity and environmental quality of the "embedded inputs" used to manufacture a particular good); allocating responsibility for a company's overall footprint (i.e. judging how much energy should be attributed to one sub-activity rather than another, related one); or optimising scientific knowledge (i.e. deciding whether an impact study should focus on company's stock of chemicals by their toxicity, sell-by date or substitution possibilities). A lack of operational knowledge can also be aggravated by the tendency within some companies to allocate insufficient resources to measurement missions.

In addition, companies can save time and money if they focus on measuring their most high-profile environmental actions instead of their less apparent ones. The problem is the subjectivity (and incentive to dissimulate) that this introduces into the process. Many environmental audits are still quite qualitative. Much work still needs to be done to hybridise them with more traditional monetary accounting practices.

Thirdly, grouping different divisions into a single balanced score-card meant to encapsulate a company's summative environmental performance is a very challenging ambition. The overarching aim of minimising environmental impacts might mean, for instance, that some divisions will focus on manufacturing efficiency (machinery, load management); others on product profiles (design features or life cycle performance); others on packaging actions (materials, recycling); and others still on company-wide resource utilisation (energy, lighting, water) or pollution generation (liquid effluents, greenhouse gases). Amalgamating such disparate "eco-audits" implies a constant risk of double accounting or, conversely, informational assumptions.

Despite these hurdles, many companies have made enormous progress in recent years towards developing truly useful environmental management systems. Of course, an EMS only really works if the vast majority of staff members commit to it, helping to design data collection systems, signify benchmarks, compare performance indicators – and above all, rethink and openly discuss all the different ways in which their individual actions contribute to the overall environmental footprint. Having said that, it bears re-stating that staff members may not always be motivated to help develop these new metrics system, with some viewing this extra task as unpaid overtime. Even worse, some employees may try to sabotage the process because of fears that tighter environmental accounting will make it harder for them to perform their jobs. Of course, it helps if everyone throughout an organisation receives psychological or material incentives to help design the new environmental metrics – encapsulated as often as not in the triple bottom-line reporting characterising modern sustainability accounting.

External reporting

As aforementioned, many companies' goal when implementing an EMS is not just to guide internal performance or monitor regulatory compliance but also (and possibly, above all) to demonstrate progress and accountability to outside stakeholders. The latter may often involve consumers worried that a company's green claims are not substantiated. On other occasions, the interested stakeholders will be investors seeking to identify the environmental aspects of a company's business model, both to judge its growth prospects and determine potential risks or liabilities. External reporting also reassures regulatory agencies and can therefore stave off more stringent controls, especially in countries where environmental disclosure is not compulsory. Lastly, a number of non-governmental organisations (NGOs) that monitor companies' sustainability profile but lack the resources to gather reliable data themselves will count on specialist bodies to provide what they hope are objective appraisals.

Companies are very aware that their reputational capital depends on the image that these and other stakeholders have of them. Where the two sides meet is in the agencies whose mission is to publicise objective third-party appraisals of members. Such agencies constitute a patchwork of bodies defined by geographic, sectorial or ethical principles. One way of categorising them is by distinguishing between reporting groups that mainly focus on processes; versus eco-labelling organisations that are more geared towards product certification.

Environmental reporting groups

Joining a body of this nature is not without risks, if only because once it happens, the company must remain a member in good standing to avoid uncomfortable questions being asked about why its standards have slipped. Moreover, companies trumpeting their environmental achievements always lay themselves open to criticism as to why they are not doing more. This, along with the costs and burdens associated with data compilation, explains why many small companies appear less willing than their larger counterparts to pay for external environmental reporting. On top of this, the proliferation of reporting groups – with each focusing on different aspects of a company's environmental promise – can create confusion and undermine the value of membership. Lastly, recurring stories about certain reporting groups' lack of diligence creates pressure on companies to only join ones with impeccable credentials. It is better for membership to allow the company to bask in a group's reflected glory than be besmirched by its poor reputation.

Different approaches have been taken to environmental reporting, depending on the needs and priorities of the parties involved. Companies are usually asked to produce an organisational mission statement delineating objectives and previous performance (expressed in quantitative but also qualitative terms indicating compliance actions). Such reports will usually contain references to the company's measurement methodology. Otherwise, it is also customary nowadays to vouch for the company's track record with affidavits signed by environmental rating agencies such as Vigeo or BMJ in France, ERM in the UK or

Innovest in the USA. Financial investors seeking to verify the sustainability credentials of a company in which they may be interested tend to focus particularly on the more technical output provided by agencies of this kind, or by the UK-based environmental research firm Trucost.

The world's largest voluntary reporting network is the UN Global Compact, which in 2019 counted nearly 10,000 corporate signatories from all across the world. Companies join the Compact to confirm their support for its basic principles, which includes, alongside environmentalism, human rights, labour standards and corruption. The environment section features three central ideas, namely that members should support a precautionary approach to environmental challenges; actively promote greater environmental responsibility; and encourage the development and diffusion of environmentally friendly technologies. The Compact can delist companies that fail to communicate progress on how they will achieve its goals. All the same, its enforcement capabilities remain relatively weak.

The world's three leading environmental reporting groups are the GRI (www.globalreporting.org/), the ISO (www.iso.org/) and the European Union's EMAS Eco-Management and Audit Scheme (http://ec.europa.eu/environment/emas/). The GRI is a large, "multi-stakeholder network" of experts promoting triple bottom-line disclosure within a "Sustainability Reporting Framework". The purpose is to give the public a full and transparent vision of the actions of its more than 13,000 reporting organisations (companies but also state agencies and NGOs). As for the ISO, its 14001 series "offers a wide-ranging portfolio of standardised sampling, testing and analytical methods to deal with specific environmental challenges [such] as the quality of air, water and soil". The ISO is a highly reputed agency that certifies corporate processes from several other perspectives as well, including labour standards and general organisational governance.

Otherwise, many sectors of activity have set up their own schemes crystallising participants' adherence to certain behavioural principles instead of requiring them to report statistical performance per se. Examples include the BSR Clean Cargo group (specialised in sustainable logistics); the International Council of Toy Industries; the International Code of Conduct on the Distribution and Use of Pesticides; and the Chlorine-Free Products Association. Similarly, the need to share knowledge about best practices has presided over the creation of a wide array of sustainability associations, ranging from open bodies like the Green Business Network (providing assistance to small- and medium-sized enterprises [SMEs]) to more ad hoc entities that members join to develop or pool their knowledge in this area.

Lastly, a host of climate change-specific reporting groups have also cropped up in recent years, reflecting the growing priority accorded to this particular concern. The question mark hanging over bodies of this kind, however, is not only how many companies are willing to divulge data but the quality of the information they provide. In green business as in other areas, statistics can be easily manipulated. Having said that, it would be unfair to cast singularly negative aspersions about the integrity of companies filing information with carbon dioxide or other environment reporting groups. The reality is that value judgements in this area, like many others, need to be nuanced. Few companies are totally good or totally bad.

Eco-labelling

Logically, consumers reacting to the claims that companies make about their own environmental virtues will be more sceptical than if these same claims have been certified by specialist labelling organisations. This is particularly important given the higher retail prices associated with many self-proclaimed green products – before spending the extra money, potential buyers will seek reassurance that they are not being taken advantage of. The net effect of these dynamics has been the rise of a number of non-profit organisations whose business proposal is the trust that consumers can have in their endorsements. The end result has been a stabilisation in the market for green goods.

Normally, eco-labelling organisations test environmental metrics similar to the ones discussed above. The kinds of factors that they might highlight include the extent to which a product is made of recycled goods (or can be recycled itself); the care taken during its production to reduce energy, water or material use; the volume of pollution (and/or non-product output) that it has generated; its climate change impact, etc. A key differentiation in this sector is between labels that simply put a stamp of approval on a product; ones that validate claimed attributes; and ones that confirm quality. Some third-party labels apply to specific companies or products, while others cover entire industries or product life cycles – one example being the 'Chain of Custody' tracking mechanism that the Germany-based FSC (Forest Stewardship Council) (www.fsc.org/) has devised. In the best of cases, trust in (and loyalty to) an eco-label can be a great catalyst for increased volumes of green business.

At the same time, eco-labelling also faces a number of problems, first and foremost being the potential for misuse if the labelling organisation facilitates misrepresentation instead of preventing it. Another challenge relates to goods whose production is fragmented across a widely dispersed international value chain. It is not at all evident that the chain's prime contractor – the one interfacing with end users – and/or the eco-labelling organisation working on its behalf will possess sufficient information on upstream suppliers' sustainability practices to guarantee a label's accuracy. This too undermines the credibility of the process.

Lastly, it is worth noting that eco-labelling is a fixed cost that can be proportionately more expensive for SMEs amortising it over smaller volumes. This has led to the rise of a number of smaller labelling bodies such as Certified Naturally Grown, which specialises in produce from small North American farms, or Ecocert in France. It also explains why some companies are trying to convince the general public that their internal metrics are as valid as any external certifications. These businesses are hoping to reduce the cost of environmental transparency by finding dual uses for information originally designed for a single purpose. By so doing, they cut the cost of going green and make the whole process more immediate.

Bibliography

Blackburn, W. (2007), *The Sustainability Handbook*, Earthscan, London.

Demirel, P. et al. (2017), "Born to be green: new insights into the economics and management of green entrepreneurship", *Small Business Economics*, Volume 52, Issue 4, pp. 759–771.

Esty, D. and Winston, A. (2009), *Green to Gold: How Smart Companies Use Environmental Strategy to Innovate, Create Value, and Build Competitive Advantage*, John Wiley & Sons, Hoboken (New Jersey).

Friend, G. (2009), *The Truth about Green Business*, FT, Upper Saddle River (New Jersey).

Hitchcock, D. and Willard, M. (2006), *The Business Guide to Sustainability: Practical Strategies and Tools for Organization*, Earthscan, London.

6　Green operations

"Tell me about spending to save"

ESSENTIAL SUMMARY

Making a company's physical operations more eco-efficient offers the benefit of both optimising its internal processes and positioning it in new technology markets. Implementing this new approach is easier said than done, however. Not only is operational greening costly, but it also requires a radical change in mindsets, with professionals now being asked to focus less on

(Continued)

output maximisation and more on input minimisation. Above all, there is the need to start viewing physical products in terms of the functionalities they offer customers, above and beyond their material attributes – essentially adding a service mission to traditional manufacturing. This is a very different approach to business operations but one that has become indispensable – if only because after so many centuries of imposing brutal synthetic production processes on sensitive natural ecosystems, continuing in the same vein would be ecologically unsustainable.

Section I. Knowledge management

The basic aim of any eco-efficient operation is to optimise material and energy inputs while minimising environmentally damaging outputs. The credo has long been recognised in business literature, dating back to the mid-20th-century writings of Buckminster Fuller, who advocated a kind of design that imitates nature and offers "more for less". At the same time, it should be noted that other thinkers have criticised eco-efficiency, accusing it of perpetuating environmental sub-performance by alleviating the negative side effects of brutal production processes instead of eliminating them altogether. In this latter view, the imperative is a wholesale reconstruction of upstream activities via a new industrial model where sustainability is embedded from the outset instead of bolted on as an afterthought – all in all, a more coherent and cheaper approach, as well as one that is easier to implement.

However, this ambition does not speak to companies' management of their enormous sunk investments in an existing industrial apparatus. Abandoning everything to facilitate a wholesale shift to more eco-efficient operational methods is prohibitively expensive. It is important to remember that for many managers, green operations will involve nothing more than designing marginal improvements to their existing assets.

Design

Green industrial design is a general term that applies as much to products as to components, packaging, manufacturing processes or any combination thereof. But whether the focus is internal or customer-facing, certain principles will always apply, starting with a preference for quality and durability over cheap materials and planned obsolescence.

One leading precept in this field is the idea that corporate operations and/or products should be designed as far as possible to imitate natural processes. Ecological literature is unanimous in its praise of eco-efficient natural systems such as forests or aquatic environments, usually characterised by biodiversity and the interdependence of component elements; by their reliance on renewable local energy inputs (or sunlight); and by waste recycling and resource husbandry. Designers implement these ideas through a variety of approaches, often relating to "biomorphism" (the imitation of intelligent patterns) or "biomimicry" (the imitation of natural functionalities).

Probably the most widely used tool in green design is William McDonough's "cradle-to-cradle" construct. The starting point here is to criticise expensive and unhealthy "end-of-product" recycling solutions – along with industrial standardisation, culpable for the mass production of contaminants. The old paradigm is then replaced with an entirely new one in which goods are conceptualised from the very outset as a function of their environmental footprint. A distinction is made between biological nutrients that can be returned seamlessly into the natural environment at the end of a product's working life, versus technical nutrients comprised of substances such as synthetic chemical compounds or other materials whose disposal poisons the ecosphere. Substances in the former category are called "products of consumption" because they can become nutrients for further life cycles after their initial usage – a safe "open loop" interaction exists between their initial manifestation as a product component and their subsequent appearance as product waste. Technical nutrients, on the other hand, are dangerous and should not be released. Instead, they should function in a "closed loop" to become reusable "products of service" fulfilling a particular design function time and again for different products or services. Obviously, the ideal is to design products that avoid toxic inputs, but if this is impossible, the key becomes the separation of biological from technical nutrients so that each can follow its own "metabolism". The fundamental advice here is for companies to correctly inventory everything that goes into their production processes – and everything that comes out. The goal is to phase out waste entirely (Figure 6.1).

Unfortunately, McDonough's vision constitutes an ideal that few companies are in a position to fully implement without abandoning their existing product ranges or production facilities. This explains why green design currently focuses more on less ambitious objectives

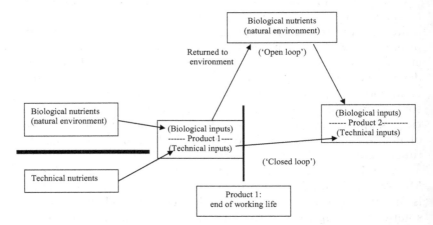

Figure 6.1 Designing for McDonough's 'Cradle-to-Cradle' Industrial Cycle.

such as reducing hazardous or other waste generated across a product's life cycle; lightweighting (using fewer materials to achieve the same outcomes); extending products' useful life via upgradeability; and facilitating end-of-life disassembly. The choice of which of these goals gets prioritised by a particular production unit depends on several factors: the company's general innovativeness and/or technical capabilities; life cycle assessments revealing the opportunity cost of greening one part of the value chain as opposed to another; the extent to which the cost of eco-efficiency investments can be passed on to customers; and whether the initiative involves new or old products. Of course, convenience is also a consideration in this arbitrage. Green design does not occur in a vacuum.

Sharing best practice is therefore essential in this effort. At times it is within the organisation that the learning will take place. More often than not, however, a company must look externally for useful design thinking, with a great many information platforms having already been created towards this end. The widespread advocacy of intelligence sharing reflects not only environmentalist ideals but also data exchanges' greater eco-efficiency (while avoiding situations where companies duplicate the same R&D activities simply because they are working their problems separately). Of course, the search for competitive advantage will undoubtedly cause many managers to want to keep discoveries secret. It remains that sharing green operational design is widely viewed as the second pillar of environmental knowledge management.

Data exchanges

There are several ways that information technology can be used to green physical operations. As aforementioned, one of the main challenges in minimising the toxicity of a company's inputs or outputs is apprehending its material flows at a granular level, a task that is particularly complicated when discussions with suppliers focus on commercial and product performance (as has historically been the case) instead of on chemical attributes. Data capabilities help at this level by inventorying substances found in a product's value chain and assessing their environmental impact from a scientific perspective that may transcend many business managers' technological capabilities. Alongside of this, an increasing number of companies have implemented environmental management systems that use information technology to better manage their logistics and inventory functions – and above all, to optimise the allocation of resources, operating much in the same way as smart grids are meant to distribute energy in the cities of the future. The idea here is to centralise information while ascertaining synergies and positive spillovers. Otherwise, data exchanges also underpin many of the environmental "balanced scorecards" that companies increasingly use to get different divisions to share best green design practice.

A special case in point is the way data exchanges can be used to address the skyrocketing energy use (and generation of e-waste) associated with data centres' growing importance to many companies. The main thought here is that companies must intensify their use of whatever computer infrastructure they possess by avoiding surplus capacities and sizing equipment to match current and future use. Alongside of this, they might also optimise electricity-hungry cooling systems by improving room layouts and inter-terminal connectivity; implement cloud computing whenever possible to reduce isolated workstations' memory requirements; and install systems that rely on LCD display technology or shut down quickly when terminals or peripherals go unused for too long.

Of course, none of this will work without user buy-in – operational greening depends not only on the definition of new processes but also on staff's willingness to adhere to them and more generally to embrace change. Given that some companies largely view the greening agenda in light of its commercial implications, there is a concern that inward-facing production staff may feel less enthusiastic about the shift to eco-efficiency than their customer-facing marketing colleagues. One of the main challenges in operational greening is to ensure that it plays out within all of a company's functional divisions.

Section II. Value chain functions

The holistic paradigm underlying all ecological thinking is best encapsulated in a construct called "industrial ecology", where an overview is taken of all of the physical operations required to make a product so as to ascertain different modalities for minimising both net resource utilisation and pollution. Some descriptions of this approach equate it with the workings of a forest, which consumes as few new inputs as possible (basically ambient sunlight and rainfall) and reuses the waste that system participants generate to sustain new life. There are multiple advantages, not only for the companies engaging in industrial ecology but also for society as a whole, if only because the paradigm emphasises localised production systems. This reduces the need for environmentally and economically expensive imports shipped from afar. At the same time, it is also clear that new value chain linkages of this sort will only be feasible if there is a modicum of coordination between participants and/or if collective infrastructure can be developed. The question then becomes who bears the cost.

As such, it is often the quality of overall coordination that determines a green value chain's chances of success. Note as well a certain number of risks associated with the adoption of a macro-organisation mainly defined by the ecological symbiosis that it creates between "co-located" industries – first and foremost being that the entire arrangement falls apart if one of the participants goes out of business or does not generate the quality or volume of waste nutrients on which its counterparts rely. Furthermore, it is not at all evident that all the by-products generated by one member of the cluster can be used by its partners, nor that companies should or will decide to locate facilities somewhere based primarily on proximity to firms with compatible waste streams. Depending on the specific level within the product value chain, other business objectives – mainly return costs – will as often as not be considered more pressing.

Upstream functions

Companies vary widely in terms of the particular value chain operation that they are most likely to try and make eco-efficient. Factors include different managers' variable commitment to green business, the sector of activity, the geographic distance between a company's subsidiaries, etc. That being the case, the most straightforward way of analysing operational greening is by going down the value chain, starting with upstream procurement activities and ending downstream with reverse logistics.

Sourcing

An operational value chain starts with the inputs (raw materials or intermediary components and modules) that companies acquire from their suppliers. Attempts to green a company's procurement operations are complicated first and foremost by the difficulty of ascertaining upstream suppliers' environmental footprint with any degree of precision, especially where hybrid products mixing different kinds of inputs are involved. This is all the harder given the international fragmentation of many supply chains today, with the many informational blind spots that this creates. Otherwise, the health and safety implications of having employees handle hazardous items – or indeed, dangerously voluminous packaging – are another reason why the sourcing function is so crucial in many operational greening initiatives.

Resolving procurement-related environmental problems requires cooperation between the companies involved in a network, often led by the prime contractor, being the party reputationally (and legally) accountable for the end product's environmental footprint. As aforementioned, cooperation can be formalised through data exchanges, involving either shared data platforms or as often as not the prime contractor imposing its own requirements on suppliers, who fear losing the account and therefore end up divulging component design or chemical composition information that they might otherwise view as confidential. Note as well that companies tend to only share their knowledge with counterparts they trust– a sentiment that largely depends on whether the supply relationship is strategic or merely transactional in nature. Otherwise, it is also possible for a system of positive or negative incentives to be set up based on suppliers' eco-performance and measured using indicators like per-pallet fuel costs (or carbon dioxide emissions). This then requires an open-book system so that all parties to the arrangement can have confidence in the figures being used.

Prescriptions of this kind are often specified in Environmentally Preferable Purchasing (EPP) contracts that generally mirror public sector procurement standards. In these arrangements, it is customary for supply contracts to contain sustainability conditions that the prime contractor will then monitor through their own EMS by doing a life cycle assessment of the goods in question. Monitoring is facilitated if the suppliers benefit from trusted environmental certification such as ISO 14001. Indeed, at advanced levels of value chain integration, some prime contractors will even sponsor "materials pools" providing the necessary green infrastructure to preferred suppliers currently unable to manufacture a given input in an environmentally friendly manner.

Manufacturing

The production of physical goods generates two footprints, one at the level of the facilities hosting the manufacturing operations and the other reflecting the actual operations themselves. Companies' main objective here will almost always be to save energy and cut costs (and/or in countries where climate change incentives systems are in place, to reduce carbon dioxide emissions). This usually entails relying on data culled from a large-scale EMS requiring an investment that is significant enough to be deemed strategic, and whose productivity will therefore be assessed using traditional financial return indicators. Note that there are a number of other, smaller steps that frontline operatives may find easier to implement in their daily routines – that is, if they are incentivised to do so by management and given the necessary information.

Companies' efforts to green their production processes can also be analysed in more conceptual terms, however. Whereas early green business analysts often focused on pollution prevention or process certification possibilities enabled by standards like ISO 14001, the talk today is more about a crossover between eco-efficient manufacturing and the industrial quality agenda – with non-product output (NPO) waste minimisation also being a priority in "lean" manufacturing paradigms such as the Toyota Production System. In this latter model, the goal is to cut overall material throughput volumes – a very eco-efficient ambition. Several mechanisms are used, including "just-in-time" inventory management, a "kaizen" search for continuous improvement and "jidoka" human automation, where operatives work to maximise quality and minimise defects. The net effect is the "rightsizing" of outputs, with manufacturing entities producing fewer but more durable good. Waste reduction and eco-efficient manufacturing mesh seamlessly with one another.

Other advances in this area translate improvements in general machine design technology, enabling devices made out of stronger, lighter and more flexible parts, hence capable of nearly zero tolerances (thereby generating less waste). Note as well the significant value chain knock-on effects when eco-efficiency innovations involve generic intermediary items destined to serve as components in a number of different end products. The effects of changes enacted during early manufacturing stages are amplified by their subsequent diffusion down the value chain (Figure 6.2).

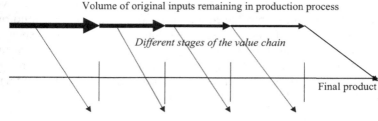

Volume of original inputs remaining in production process

Different stages of the value chain

Final product

Dissipation of original inputs (consumed in process or rejected as waste)
= Accumulation of "non-products"

Figure 6.2 Non-Product Ratios Rise as Goods Are Transformed into Final Products.

Downstream functions

Many operational greening efforts are stimulated by downstream commercial concerns about a company's environmental reputation, especially in cases where the public worries that the physical processes it undertakes may have toxic effects. Companies will sometimes pre-empt criticism by taking it upon themselves to remove toxic substances from their products and replacing them with harmless substitutes. Of course, the success of this action also depends whether customers and other stakeholders trust the company making these changes. In green operations as in other areas, public perception is key to commercial success.

Packaging

One of the most visible problems in global waste management today is the mountain of packaging generated by modern production and consumption patterns. Packaging is an upstream topic when it relates to shipments of raw materials and industrial components – although an assumption can be made that such operations are largely utilitarian in nature and tend to be pared down to their functional attributes. At the downstream interface with end users, however, there is a longstanding pattern of companies viewing product packaging as a marketing tool, thereby wasting vast quantities of paper and other wrappings for nothing better than aesthetic reasons (or to enhance consumers' product confidence). Having said that, improvements in this area are relatively easier to achieve than elsewhere. Indeed, many companies have used packaging reduction schemes to kickstart their operational greening drives.

Fundamentally, the main ways that companies can diminish the net volume of the packaging they produce is to intensify the use of recycled, biodegradable or bio-based materials and create designs (and/or incentive schemes, like deposit returns) that help consumers dispense with packaging altogether. Conversely, there is an argument in favour of sturdier packaging that can be reused, sometimes after cleaning. Above all, there are widespread efforts made throughout the modern industry to design less packaging for any given product volume.

Logistics

Value chains are affected at every level by the logistics function, which integrates different stages in what is sometimes called global supply chain management. Categorising this activity as downstream is somewhat arbitrary, and it is important to remember that the earlier stages in a product's overall manufacturing process might represent the final customer interface for companies specialising in upstream inputs. As such, it is often helpful to apply a relatively broad term like "distribution" when describing goods' general physical movements.

To a certain extent, distribution volumes (amount of goods transported and the distances involved) reflect other strategic decisions made by companies. First and foremost is their chosen configuration – namely whether manufacturing units are situated close to supply sources or consumer markets; if a central transportation hub approach is being used (instead of direct hence diverse transport flows); and whether production is being outsourced locally or internationally. Multinational enterprises that have opted for dispersed configurations will necessarily have a greater distribution footprint. For agricultural products, this is encapsulated in the construct of food miles – a topical debate pitting the ecological imperative versus many emerging economies' development priorities.

Reducing companies' logistics or distribution footprint generally involves two kinds of actions. First, at an industrial level, shipments can be redesigned to weigh less. More strategically, increasing the interchangeability of supplies or parts can reduce the overall need for transportation. Second and above all, against today's general backdrop of rising fuel prices, saturated infrastructure and pollution concerns, the transportation sector itself has become a major battleground for operational improvements. It is here that many companies encounter their first eco-efficiency challenges, irrespective of whether they own their own transportation fleet or, increasingly, outsource the function to specialist third-party logistics providers – who will then mix ("commingle") different customers' shipments to avoid environmentally inefficient partial loads. Logistics specialists are responsible for many headline green innovations because the services they provide are so energy-dependent and polluting. Examples include vehicle operators' increasing implementation of telematics software to manage fleet use; "right-sizing" vehicles to match load sizes; reducing idling time and re-routing itineraries in a way that will cut both fuel usage and; greenhouse gas emissions.

The final operation then is reverse logistics – also known as recycling. The seminal principle in all green business is that products which cannot be reused at the end of their working lives are wasteful hence costly, if not to the company itself then to society (and the ecosphere) as a whole. Yet setting up functional recycling systems can be quite challenging. On the one hand, market prices for recyclates do not always justify this activity in purely financial terms. On the other, many items (such as plastics or paper) tend to lose some of their flexibility or strength attributes when recycled and can only be restored through the addition of chemicals that are not only costly but environmentally damaging, largely defeating the purpose of the whole exercise. In addition, there is the aforementioned technical difficulty of processing mixed waste streams combining biological with technical nutrients. Lastly, this whole topic is affected by the uncertainty surrounding the legal liabilities that companies increasingly face under "extended stewardship" regimes extending their responsibility past the end of their products' working lives.

Despite all this, recycling has become one of the most iconic of all operational greening activities. Sometimes the tone is set by government policy, one example being Germany's *Duales System Deutschland* (DSD) scheme requiring all companies to develop recycling schemes for any packaging they produce. This would be prohibitively expensive if companies paid for the entire operation themselves – especially where high volume, mass goods are concerned. The answer has been the establishment of an alternative *Grüner Punkt* green dot system where companies pay a licensing fee reflecting the variable costs of recycling different material streams before mandating DSD to collect the waste on their behalf. Note that putting a green dot on packaging has the added benefit of reminding customers that the company in question is helping to fund the national recycling system – a sign of good corporate citizenship that often produces a reputational advantage.

On other occasions, it is economics that drives a company's recycling efforts, specifically when older components are used to "remanufacture" goods. This has become big business in some cases, Operations of this sort – which, by their very nature, satisfy green engineers' preference for closed-loop solutions – are enabled when the product components in question are designed from the very outset to facilitate end-of-life disassembly. This can include labelling parts for easier identification or engineering them to be functionally interchangeable. Lastly, in some consumer product sectors, the key to piquing customers' interest in recycling small, low-value items is to convert sales counters into collection points. This has the added benefit of allowing companies to display their eco-efficiency credentials directly to customers and by so doing reveal the intimate value chain links that exist between green operations and green marketing.

Bibliography

Achillas, C. et al. (2018), *Green Supply Chain Management*, Routledge, Abingdon (UK).

Braungart, M. and McDonough, W. (2002), *Cradle to Cradle. Remaking the Way We Make Things*, North Point Press, New York.

Darnall, N. and Edwards, D. (2006), "Predicting the cost of environmental management system adoption: the role of capabilities, resources and ownership structure", *Strategic Management Journal*, Volume 27, Issue 4, pp. 301–320.

Pieyck, M. ed. (2015), *Green Logistics: Improving the Environmental Sustainability of Logistics*, 3rd edition, Kogan, Philadelphia.

Yale School of Forestry and Environmental Studies, *Journal of Industrial Ecology*, https://onlinelibrary.wiley.com/journal/15309290

7 Green marketing

"Message: the impossible is always possible"

ESSENTIAL SUMMARY

Marketing analysts have long been aware of the ostensible contradiction between environmentalism and mass consumption. This reflects the basic conflict between the anti-materialist values that have traditionally animated the green movement and the material definition of success prevailing in many consumerist societies today. The effect is often to marginalise green marketing from the outset, thereby undermining its credibility.

(Continued)

Such scepticism is understandable at one level. For consumers facing a purchasing decision, the environmental consequences of their act are usually of secondary importance at best. Conversely, many environmentalists are averse to a kind of marketing that, while proclaiming a company's good intentions, still induces people to consume ever greater quantities of material goods, sparking further resource depletion and pollution. Until these dilemmas are resolved, green marketing will struggle to become mainstream.

Section I. Green consumption

Since one of the main goals of any marketing effort is to implant in consumers' minds the idea that a business shares their values (and that they can therefore feel at ease with themselves when purchasing its goods), companies necessarily struggle when marketing green business to consumers who are oblivious to environmentalism. The question then becomes how to target both the relatively few customers who are already attuned to this agenda and the many others who have yet to find it relevant to their consumer behaviour.

The problem here is that different consumer groups find different things relevant at different times. For instance, since the late 20th century, growing numbers of consumers have signalled a desire to align their purchasing acts with a sense of social responsibility. The idea that economic actors might be driven by altruistic attitudes has led to the rise of "social" marketing where companies highlight the social and environmental benefits of doing business with them (Figure 7.1).

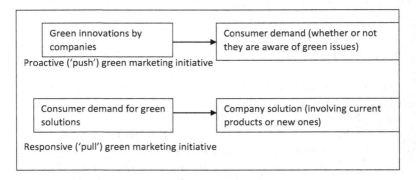

Figure 7.1 Impetus behind Green Marketing Efforts.

Segmenting green consumers

Social marketing induces potential consumers to look beyond their immediate material self-interest and consider the longer-term communitarian impacts of their purchasing decisions. By so doing, however, the approach creates a conflict between self-interest and group-interest that is akin, in psychological terms, to the divide between the id and the superego. Such confusion is particularly unsettling when the promises being made seem distant, either in time or in place. One major challenge for green marketing is educating consumers to favour products offering long-term benefits that accrue to distant populations instead of short-term benefits that accrue to themselves. Indeed, there is much debate whether this can be accomplished without a revolutionary shift in global cultural values.

The first hurdle is the absence of knowledge about which populations tend to consume green products and why they do this. The picture is mixed where gender is concerned, with women appearing to be the main green consumers in certain countries and men in others (revealing the need for a very granular level of market segmentation). At the same time, certain commonalities do exist between segments, reflecting convergence effects that marketing gurus like Theodore Levitt have long identified. In general, there is evidence the green consumers tend to be older, wealthier and better educated than the average consumer. Less price-sensitive and more apt to feel loyalty to a particular brand or store, they shop more frequently and buy larger quantities. In short – and contrary to popular mythology – many green consumers display characteristics that are very much at odds with the monk-like or hippy qualities commonly attributed to them.

Clearly, social and/or green marketing will be more effective with consumers whose internal value systems view the satisfaction of community and personal needs as being equally rewarding. Thus, there is also a strong generational aspect of green consumption. The problem is that younger generations with an abstract interest in green purchasing also have tighter budgets. Of course, over time and as these populations' purchasing power increase, there should be a concomitant rise in solvent demand for green products.

Green intentions vs. green purchases

Companies often face consumers who have been somewhat sensitized to environmental problems (and may have a vague desire to do something about them) but remain unwilling or unable to translate this into concrete purchases. There is a significant slippage between the number of consumers who would ideally like to buy green products, the number familiar with actual products, the number actually looking for them in-store, the number actually finding them, and the number actually buying them. There are several reasons for this slippage, including a general lack of information about green alternatives; insufficient assortments; suboptimal in-store locations or point-of-sale communications; and, above all, the fact that many customers lack an initial "willingness-to-pay" a premium for specifically green products.

These obstacles can only be overcome if customers receive assurances that the green product will perform as well as the traditional alternative while also fulfilling whatever other promises it makes. This is a significant hurdle, particularly where hyperbolic "greenwash" marketing has aggravated potential consumers' cynicism. Otherwise, many customers also have availability concerns, presuming that because green products are not sold everywhere they will be harder to find in sufficient quantities and should therefore not be considered reliably replenishable staples. Last but not least comes the significant hurdle of price, being the difference between the "normal" surcharge that budding green consumers might expect to pay and the high sticker prices charged by retailers seeking to maximise margins on novelty items. It is important to note that with few exceptions, green products tend to be sold at a premium, either because their innovation costs (and absence of industrial scale) warrant a mark-up or because sellers want to take advantage of their rarity value. This price constraint is a constant factor in green marketing. Customers who are already amenable to green arguments might take it in stride, but for everyone else, the obstacle can be insurmountable.

Section II. Green marketing choices

Some consumer segments appear naturally more inclined to proactively demand green solutions. They contrast with other less engaged segments, where the impetus for green marketing must come from the company itself. This distinction between companies "pushing" a new message or being "pulled" in by market signals is a key dividing line in both international and green business analysis.

"Push" vs. "pull" marketing

A responsive "pull" strategy almost always has a greater chance of success due to the fact that the promised benefits correspond to preferences that the market has already made explicit. At the same time, a company's rivals will also pick up on these signals, making it harder to charge a green premium. Such strategies therefore tend to cover high-volume/low-return/low-risk commodity products. Conversely, in proactive "push" marketing, the company is in a position to achieve a first mover advantage with its new green idea and can therefore charge a higher price. Of course, because the innovator can never be sure whether the product will resonate among potential buyers, proactive initiatives also tend to fail more often, i.e. the approach is characterised by low volume/high return/high risk. Having said that, companies proactively positioning themselves as green innovators are also more likely to benefit from a halo effect because their first-mover status helps to define a positive image in consumers' eyes. This partially offsets the greater risk associated with "push" efforts.

With many market segments remaining relatively ignorant of green business, companies often feel that they have no other choice than to pursue a "push" approach in this field. The first step then becomes educating potential consumers about the benefits of green consumption. This can be psychologically quite difficult, however. Lacking previous knowledge on how innovative green products work, potential buyers' initial reaction will often be one of incredulity. The degree of resistance that companies encounter at this level depends on whether the consumer is being asked to accept a green product that produces specific quantifiable benefits, or a green brand, which is a more emotive choice (Figure 7.2).

Companies can overcome reactions of incredulity with messages containing at least one element familiar to potential customers. For consumers – especially in the Lifestyles of Health and Sustainability (LOHAS) segment – new green products' health-related benefits can

	Companies marketing a green product	Companies marketing a green brand
Consumers already sensitized to the ecological imperative	Responsive 'pull': volume markets driven by competitive arguments such as price	Responsive 'pull': company hopes for 'halo effect' helping to sell other products
Consumers not yet sensitized to the ecological imperative	Proactive 'push': argument focused on material benefits such as lower 'lifecycle' costs	Proactive 'push': long-term project to educate potential future customers

Figure 7.2 Examples of Green Marketing Segmentation.

fit the bill. On other occasions, the company will want to make life cycle assessment (LCA) arguments, asking potential buyers to reason in terms of the long-term savings that the product generates. Because this is more of an intellectual argument than an emotional one, however, its potential use is limited in mass consumer markets. On the other hand, intellectual green arguments are likely to be better received in business-to-business (B2B) sectors where the customers are themselves professionals and therefore more accustomed to thinking in LCA terms.

Green marketing mix

From their general programme, business students will be familiar with standard marketing mix parameters such as product, price, promotion, place (the "four p's"). The section below applies these tools in a specifically environmental context.

Green products

There are various ways of categorising green products. One is to distinguish between items that generate no direct environmental benefits themselves but are manufactured according to environmental principles – as opposed to products whose green benefits are realised by the end user upon consumption. Other comparators include products' health and safety profile; the amount of waste (including packaging) they generate; or, as aforementioned, their LCA. Different green arguments will have varying impacts on different target markets, depending as well on whether the marketing involves B2B or business to consumers (B2C) efforts.

Lastly, there is also a difference between marketing green consumer perishables vs. durables – with the latter being conducive to messaging that appeals simultaneously to consumers' emotions (trendiness) and rationality (lower LCA, reduced energy consumption). The psychology associated with green perishables also differs from green durables since the benefits accrue mainly to buyers themselves and not society as a whole. Consumers often see perishables as very personal items, an intimacy slightly at odds with the more collective ethos that is an intrinsic part of green marketing's generally altruistic emphasis. This personalisation should have the effect of making the act of purchasing green perishables less unusual, in the sense that it actually speaks to people's self-interest much in the same way as the equivalent non-green goods do. It is for this reason that some of the earliest green products to have experienced mass success (such as organic food or natural cosmetics) are found in this category.

Green pricing

Green products' generally higher point-of-sale price partially reflects the fact that many companies take advantage of the items' novelty value to impose premium pricing. Also, few green products will have achieved sufficient production scale to lower unit costs and achieve economies of scale. Lastly, many have fundamentally higher return costs due to the care taken during their manufacturing phase to use higher quality inputs, internalise the cost of any waste generated and provide reverse logistics facilities enabling end-of-life recycling.

At the same time, price competition is not always considered paramount in green business. Quite the contrary, there is a greater focus in this area on ensuring that all of the environmental costs associated with a good's sourcing, transformation, commercialisation and ultimate disposal are fully accounted for in its price. Unlike their non-green rivals, green products are supposed to incorporate all the ecological costs incurred not only by the company making and selling them but also by society as a whole. Where price alone is concerned, this generally puts them at a competitive disadvantage.

Selling expensive goods implies niche positioning since consumers will only migrate to the new product if they can afford to and if something helps them overcome the price barrier. Even among consumers segments with an existing interest in green products (and who can afford them), the higher retail price is an obstacle that will only be overcome if consumers' psychological state at the time of the purchase lends itself to this. Yet consumer populations characterised by an inelastic demand to price are few and far between. The question is whether this condemns green products to a permanent minority status.

Companies marketing green products must pursue specific avenues to overcome the price disadvantage. The most direct approach involves organising point-of-sale promotions reminding potential purchasers why they should be willing to pay more. Such efforts will be most effective if they mix emotional, brand and/or cause-related appeals with more reasoned arguments detailing concrete benefits. All these registers can be useful, and indeed might be necessary where products cost a significant green premium.

Intuitively it seems clear that the higher a green product's price premium, the greater people's reluctance to buy it. The extent of this reluctance to pay extra – and conversely, the size of the surcharge that people are willing to pay – will depend on the product in question. Different factors come into play at this level: consumers' cultural values and demographic characteristics, prevailing socioeconomic conditions, the extent to which consumers have already been educated in LCA valuations, etc.

A good example of the kind of LCA education that helps consumers to overcome the green premium price barrier is the way that many solar heating companies prepare potential buyers psychologically before revealing their systems' considerable price tags. Marketing communications in this area often start with in-depth analyses of environmental problems (global warming, rising fuel prices) followed by a discussion of potential targets' current energy bills and resource consumption behavior; an evaluation of possible future bills based on energy price forecasts; and calculations identifying the long-term savings that can be achieved by switching to solar. It is only at the end of this long process that the new system's price is revealed. This approach reduces the psychological shock from which potential green customers are bound to suffer when discovering the high initial outlay that they are being asked to make.

Different factors affect people's mindset in a purchasing situation. One is the persuasion work that the company does to prepare the moment. Another is the physical (or virtual) context of the place in which the purchase takes place. This latter factor explains why "place" is the third parameter in the marketing mix toolbox.

Green places

Given green marketing's anti-gigantism ethos and antipathy to huge out-of-town shopping centres, it is unsurprising that green retail originally centred on small local stores or cooperatives often staffed by environmental devotees trying to escape the corporate lifestyle. Even today, specialist outlets still account for a disproportionately large percentage of all green product sales. They are no longer as dominant as they used to be, however, with almost all of the world's leading retail chains starting to offer green product ranges to a greater or lesser extent. Whether these ranges are interspersed with non-green goods in store sections defined by product category, or sold separately in dedicated green (or organic) sections, depends if management's main priority is normalise customer transition to green consumption or to sharpen the store's reputation as a green provider.

Green retailing has also developed a number of idiosyncratic distribution channels.

Guerrilla marketing. In this case, big-budget campaigns based on high-profile mass media vehicles are replaced by small but innovative and targeted local efforts that, in line with environmentalism's proximity ethos, fit directly into consumers' standard day-to-day routines. In effect, this approach involves marketing specialists applying eco-friendly principles (like zero waste "clean advertising" methods) to their own medium.

Insofar as the Internet can be viewed as a non-traditional advertising medium, it is possible to conceive of all online communications as a form of green guerrilla marketing. Certainly, many green communications specialists prefer to operate online. This can involve the viral marketing of environmentally friendly brands or offering the kinds of sustainability sections found on many if not most large companies' websites today. There is also the way that environmentalists use guerrilla marketing actions to mobilise crowds – exemplified in "carrot-mobbing" actions where groups of shoppers arrange online to descend all at once on a store they want to support because it is taking steps to reduce its environmental footprint. Success stories like this one bolster optimists' view that companies should view environmentalism first and foremost as an opportunity to re-define their business models in a way that directly benefits the bottom line.

Online green marketing can be used to publicise not only physical retail outlets but also e-commerce, which can reasonably claim to produce many green benefits – starting with the resources that buyers and sellers save by avoiding in-store purchasing, which generates transportation costs for customers and inventory and operating costs for retailers. Similarly, e-commerce may require less packaging and paper than traditional physical merchandising, in part because goods are delivered directly from the warehouse to the end user. It is also possible to argue that online marketing is more coherent with green values since the messages are being diffused via resource-thrifty web-based solutions instead of using paper.

Shared platform experiences. Often web-based but also occurring in non-virtual (i.e. physical) spaces, this kind of marketing involves green consumers coming together specifically to enact certain environmental principles. The aim is generally to minimise waste and reduce consumption by sharing services and/or recycling. Rooted in a collaborative ethos, these are often small- and medium-sized schemes where monetary transactions – asides from the organisers pocketing small membership fees as a reward for hosting and marketing the service – play a lesser role than they usually do. Examples include the growing number of non-profit municipal auto and bike-share schemes where members book a vehicle for a limited period of time.

Because such schemes are self-directed and usually not very lucrative, few are of much interest to big corporations. At the same time, by using this approach to build brand tribes, companies can foster potential customers' self-awareness as green consumers, laying foundations for a sense of identity that might subsequently turn into a commercial relationship.

Eco-sponsoring of this kind is one of the most efficient tools used in proactive approaches where, as aforementioned, the impetus for the green business comes from the company itself. It can also be categorised as a kind of green promotion – the final and probably most widely discussed parameter in the (green) marketing mix toolbox.

Green promotions

In a world where some multinational enterprises' revenues exceed the gross domestic product of entire national economies – thus where the consequences of corporate action extend far beyond the commercial domain alone – over the long run companies can only truly legitimise their power if they can be viewed as responsible members of the communities in which they operate. Green marketing sends out concrete signals that a company is not only cognizant of stakeholders' ecological concerns but also proactive about improving the environment. This attitude has been shown to have real benefits for a company's brand image, thus its bottom line. It enhances overall reputational capital and helps consolidate existing consumers' loyalty.

In a pure marketing sense, however, promotion refers to a whole range of communications initiatives, including point-of-sale actions, internal corporate communications and external advertising. It is this latter aspect that is most apparent to (and has the greatest effect on) potential green consumers.

Back in the early 1990s, as more and more companies began promoting their green credentials, expressions like "bio-degradable" and even "recyclable" or "refillable" were relatively new and would often be overused and/or misused by companies. In turn, this sparked a move in several countries towards greater regulation of green advertising. The oversight remains patchy, however, meaning that exaggerated and sometimes false green claims still persist. Such behaviour has undermined green promotions' credibility among many potential customers, reinforcing their reluctance to buy green goods. The problem is further aggravated if the target audience suffers "green fatigue" after being overly solicited with environmental messages.

Given the other obstacles that green marketing faces, companies cannot afford this added hurdle of scepticism. One way that they have tried to overcome it is through eco-labelling. The crucial factor at this level is that the environmental message be crafted in a way that fits specific circumstances. Companies can appeal to consumers' rationality, social responsibility, subjectivity and/or material interest. The effectiveness of each emphasis will vary both in time and place and also depending on whether the tonality that the company uses is viewed as appropriate to the product and the circumstances.

Environmental messages tend to indicate different combinations of strategic positioning. For instance, a company with a damaged green reputation in need of repair might choose to combine a green brand focus with appeals to the wider social benefits of environmentally friendly behaviour. Conversely, companies seeking to overcome their neophyte status in the field of sustainability might choose to highlight their brands' green credentials while appealing to consumer self-interest. Note that this kind of positioning generally combines generic social branding with a personalised green promise. This is because the complexity of green marketing often requires newcomers to play on several registers simultaneously to get consumers' attention.

Product-specific advertising identifying green benefits for society as a whole tends to be used by companies offering a more expensive range of goods or services, and who therefore have less chance of appealing to consumers' value-for-money self-interest. The register is also appropriate for brands that are already well entrenched with their customer base. At times, green promotion involves less of a radical shift in focus and more the consolidation and extension of a company's current marketing positioning.

Lastly, product-specific green advertising focused on consumer self-interest is often found in saturated markets where differentiation requires as personal a promise as possible. This is because personalised promises often seem more credible with a product that is intimate to an individual, and/or where the target segment has not been identified as being particularly sensitive to altruistic arguments.

The above categorisation is not exhaustive, largely because hybrid positions are always possible. For example, companies may need to position themselves in a certain way in some markets but differently elsewhere. There are also situations where a company will promote some of its products as being green – but not all. To some extent, promoting non-green images is a luxury that can only be afforded by companies which have already consolidated a sufficiently green reputation.

Consumers' receptiveness to a green promotion will also depend on the extent to which they view it as fact-based or, conversely, as manipulative. This wariness is very much part of the zeitgeist of cynicism characterising many modern consumers. It has been encapsulated in a new marketing construct – the "99 to 1" rule, or the accusation that some companies devote 99 percent of their promotional efforts to green product lines that constitute a mere 1 percent of their actual portfolio. It is cognitively confusing for consumers to believe in companies (or products) that are green in a few respects and non-green in most others. Such confusion has led to a rising number of complaints to regulatory watchdogs worldwide about instances of greenwashing. The end effect has been to undermine general belief in the sincerity of green marketing – a decidedly bad idea given all the other obstacles that companies must overcome in this area.

Bibliography

Ginsberg, J. and Bloom, P. (2004), "Choosing the right green marketing strategy", *MIT Sloan Management Review*, Fall, Volume 46, Issue 1, pp. 79–84.

GMA and Deloitte (2009), "Finding the Green in Today's Shoppers Sustainability Trends and New Shopper Insights", https://www.gmaonline.org/downloads/research-and-reports/greenshopper09.pdf

Grant, J. (2007), *The Green Marketing Manifesto*, John Wiley & Sons, Chichester (UK).

Peattie, K. and Charter, M. (2003), "Green marketing", Baker, M. (ed.), *The Marketing Book*, 5th edition, Butterworth-Heinemann, pp. 726–755.

Sheehan, K. and Atkinson, L. (2014), *Green Advertising and the Reluctant Customer*, Routledge, Abingdon (UK).

8　Green growth sectors

"Things can only get better"

ESSENTIAL SUMMARY

Entrepreneurial interest in green business opportunities can be ascertained in different ways. One is by monitoring patent registrations, although questions remain about the comparability of national data and, above all, how much time a patent takes to translate into an industrial application. More generally, there are already several benchmark information sources regularly producing exhaustive reports on global trading conditions in sectors ripe for an expansion of green business initiatives.

(Continued)

One widespread prediction today is that within a few short years resource productivity will become the main driver of global economic growth. The United Nations itself expects that up to 24 million new green jobs will be created between 2019 and 2030.

At the same time and depending on how green business initiatives are being channelled, different rollout scenarios might be envisaged. A useful way of organising analysis in this regard is around sectors since it is at this level that new technologies and managerial paradigms spawn new production organisations, achieve critical mass and ultimately diffuse.

Section I. Staples

However far humankind has advanced over the millennia, a hierarchy of bodily needs must still be satisfied before other considerations can be addressed. This starts with food and drink, two staples without which life is impossible.

Agriculture

Following the Green Revolution of the 1960s, global food markets experienced nearly half a century during which the planet – with the notable exception of certain highly indebted poor countries – enjoyed an increasing abundance of food. Benefiting from technological progress and government support, the Global North's agricultural output soon exceeded global consumption needs, despite the world population rising from three billion in 1970 nearly eight billion in 2020. The ensuing food surpluses flooded many markets, putting downwards pressure on prices and forcing farmers to restore profit margins by implementing increasingly intensive agricultural methods. This led to an overuse of fertilisers and pesticides, impoverishing arable land worldwide. Add to this water stresses resulting from population growth, over-irrigation and recurring drought, and it becomes clear that staples like food and water are the two sectors where environmental interests and business interests are very closely linked.

The early 21st century saw a historic reversal in the food markets' long-standing trend towards higher surpluses and lower prices. The explanation for this is simply that demand rose far more quickly than supply – by itself, always a promising situation for producers (Figure 8.1).

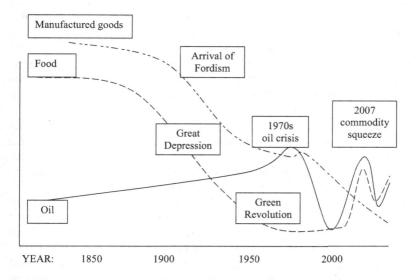

Figure 8.1 Different Sectors' Relative Pricing over Time.

On the demand side, the more than twofold rise in global population over previous decades was always likely to drive food prices much higher in the absence of an equivalent rise in productivity and output. The effects were amplified, however, by "food globalisation". This refers to the changed preferences of many Global South consumers, once their standard of living had improved enough to allow them to seek foodstuffs (specifically meat and dairy products) more elaborate than their previously basic diets. The problem is that this constitutes a comparatively wasteful use of primary food since a great deal of edible grain must be fed to livestock for them to produce the same amount of energy as people can get from simply eating plant grains directly.

Even more wasteful is the food culture that has long reigned in the Global North, reflecting comfortable consumers' rich diet and habit of buying (or having supermarkets stock) more food than is actually needed, with surpluses simply being thrown away. Note that this practice has also spawned a number of green business opportunities for green business already, starting with leaner logistics systems enabling just-in-time deliveries and including packaging and recycling innovations.

On the supply side, a number of other factors come into play, first and foremost being land taken out of production either due to nutrient depletion caused by overuse or because climate conditions have deteriorated to the extent of turning previously fertile fields into quasi-arid deserts. The effects are compounded by ever-increasing competition for land, exemplified by the destruction of farmland through urban sprawl, not to mention certain farmers' replacement of food with biofuel production. A further worry is that such practices, involving new crops being planted in virginal fields, will aggravate climate change by releasing currently embedded carbon dioxide (similar to when tropical rainforests are cut down).

The extended application of international division of labour principles to the global food industry has also had a supply-side effect. As has happened in other sectors, agriculture has witnessed greater specialisation in recent decades, with a number of countries making a proactive choice to only produce certain monocultures, hence accepting to import everything else. One of the outcomes of the globally fragmented supply chains resulting from this has been the rising power of food sector distributors, who amortise the delivery systems they set up by ignoring local seasonality and offering the same products all year around. This not only racks up environmentally damaging "food miles" but adds to the sector's overall dependence on transport (hence energy) prices, already a concern for farmers because of the way it affects equipment but also fertiliser costs.

It is true that a number of sustainable agricultural initiatives have arisen in recent years to face these challenges. Some start with farmers' social protection, seeking to enhance overall resilience to agricultural stress by empowering human capital through the diffusion of better technology and resource husbandry techniques. Others look to fill the gap between rural agriculture and urban consumption, in line with ideas formulated by visionaries such as Dickson Despommier, whose "vertical farm" concept encourages architects to design buildings with "edible walls" that inhabitants can use to grow their own produce. City planners have also started to target similar outcomes by creating "transition towns" characterised by a seamless interpenetration of urban and agricultural land use. Shortening production–consumption channels will also have the added benefit of promoting biodiversity.

Agriculture by its very nature has always been – and will likely remain – marked by the alignment of finance and ecology. Some innovations here are widespread but contested – one example being the arrival of genetically modified (GM) strains that may be hardy but whose biological effects are uncertain (and where seed productions is monopolised by a few multinational enterprises). Other opportunities, like the rising popularity of organic local produce, can be attractive but are limited to small niches. A big hope for the future is rising productivity in South Russia's former collective farms and above all in Africa, where technological progress and land reforms could readily produce much higher yields. The territorial scales involved mean, however, that larger companies will be in a better position to take advantage of these opportunities.

Of course, as always in green business, the main hurdle will be cost. A partial re-localisation of food supply chains could have an environmentally beneficial effect, but this may entail certain farming activities returning to the Global North where costs are much higher. Otherwise, localisation creates diseconomies of scale compared to the current system of focusing agricultural production on as few mega-sites as possible. The irony is that small farmers who might be interested in positioning themselves in sustainable local niches may not have the resources to do so, whereas large conglomerates who can afford it might lack the motivation.

Water

Like agriculture, the problems besetting the global water sector can be largely divided between supply and demand factors. In terms of the former, the main stress nowadays is the aforementioned recurrence of global warming-related drought. This is a worldwide phenomenon affecting all continents to a greater or lesser extent. The exact scenario for the future is difficult to determine since climate change is likely to translate into more rainfall in certain places (which may reduce general awareness the problem) and less in others (having the opposite effect). Clearly, any adjustment – like moving vast populations escaping newly desertified zones – will be arduous.

Population growth and proximity to water used to be correlated. The long-distance transportation of water supplies – involving the construction of aquifers and/or a global bottled water market (hence devastating plastics pollution) – seems to have loosened this connection, as witnessed by large-scale migrations to many of the world's normally more arid regions. For communities to survive in these naturally hostile environments, a number of governments have started to invest in desalination, a terribly energy-intensive industrial activity that also causes great damage to local wetlands. Policymakers worldwide are frequently advised by bodies such as the International Water Association to expend greater sums on water infrastructure, reducing losses from leaky pipes, protecting natural reservoirs from pollution and diffusing rainwater harvesting processes. This is especially crucial in Global South countries whose development trajectories are often undermined by households' lack of access to potable water sources. Given the scale of the gap between supply and demand in the future, however, there are serious doubts that simple efficiency measures will suffice. Thus – and as is so often the case in environmental matters – the only real hope is for a slowdown in demand. The complication for water selling companies is that on the face of things, this recommendation is not good for profits. For companies developing water-saving products, on the other hand, the prospects are excellent.

Note as well that water is used for many commercial purposes, ranging from power generation (dams and hydroelectric power) to industrial cooling and cleaning. Above all, it is used for agriculture, which accounts for the lion's share of global water consumption and is therefore the sector where most can be done to increase water productivity. This is a challenge, however, given the water-intensive nature of many crops. As happens so often in green business, the solution to one problem creates a new one.

A slew of urban and/or industrial initiatives have been launched to address water scarcity. Many relate to building design and are based on actions such as the installation of water supply control and repair systems, high-efficiency fixtures (toilets, faucets) and smart meters monitoring total on-site use. More structurally, there is some hope that urban consumption can be lowered if users move from centralised to localised systems via techniques like rainwater harvesting. Also noteworthy are the measures taken by a number of industrial companies to improve water efficiency (treatment of wastewater, recycling of runoffs, etc.). Unfortunately, there is often a sense that these steps deal with the symptoms of the problem rather than its causes.

Section II. Habitat sectors

After sustenance, the second basic human need is "habitat", a broad concept that encompasses the different structures organising physical human interactions: where they live and how they get around. A third component – energy – is of such importance to green business that it will be analysed on its own in a separate, final chapter.

Green construction

The construction industry is comprised of myriad sub-sectors, each with its own environmental profile. One is the lighting sector, accounting in some countries for around one-third of all electricity used in buildings. Another is building materials. Few companies are in a position to specialise in all of these competencies, meaning that construction projects are often driven by consortia of partner firms. The question this raises is to what extent partners have similar environmental expectations or performance.

The first distinction to make in green construction is between existing and new build. Many developers nowadays are compelled by state authorities to apply green construction principles either directly to the structures that they are building (materials, installed technology) and/or to the surrounding infrastructure (i.e. combined heat and power [CHP] facilities). These principles are relatively straightforward in new projects. However, retrofitting older units built to pre-ecological specifications is much more difficult, hence expensive. In this sector as in others, the more a green solution is applied ex post facto instead of being incorporated into the design process from the very outset, the harder it will be to implement.

The principles underlying green construction are worth reviewing. Buildings have a significant environmental footprint during both their construction and operational phases. A leading concern in the former area is the production of traditional concrete. Hence, the ambitious work being done to develop a concrete capable of sequestering carbon dioxide emissions – including a move towards biophilic building design approaches using trees or other natural elements such as roof gardens to maintain temperatures, produce oxygen and sequester carbon. The goal here is to create a healthy environment healing the "sick building" syndrome affecting many users today. Similarly, there is a new emphasis on empowering buildings' occupants to control their micro-environments via thermostats, smart meters and other tools and energy management systems instead of the heavy-handed traditional practice of blasting vast quantities of heated or cooled air indiscriminately throughout the structure. Today's architects talk about humanising people's experience of being indoors.

Strong codes have demonstrably been a real fillip for green construction. The benchmark in this area is a standard formulated by the United States Green Building Council and widely referred to as LEED or Leadership in Energy and Environmental Design. LEED covers a range of building projects (New Construction, Existing Buildings, Commercial Interiors, etc.) and features a variety of performance levels. The question then becomes which will be applied where – an arbitrage based on companies' cost vs. reputation arbitrages, not to mention wide international variations in green building standards.

Alongside these overarching building codes, a number of targeted efficiency standards also exist, including well-known certifications like Energy Star that can apply either to whole buildings or to parts thereof. Buildings worldwide are undergoing greening processes but to varying extents, with some projects involving simultaneous improvements in several areas (lighting, appliances, equipment, temperature control, etc.) and others being more narrowly defined. Note as well a distinction between the kind of greening work done during an initial construction phase (materials used, etc.) or during subsequent operational phases (energy consumption, maintenance, cleaning, etc.).

There are several reasons for the rapid spread of green construction. On the one hand, the prospect of future energy price rises provides a strong market incentive for buyers to pay the surcharge required for more energy-efficient buildings. Otherwise national economic stimulus packages increasingly favour wide-scale retrofitting and weather-proofing programmes. A whole range of businesses – from eco-equipment manufacturers to post-construction eco-performance auditors – benefit from this new focus, culminating in entirely new product lines like Passiv- and Aktivhaus designs. Significantly, both the construction and the energy sector have a stake in such projects. The fact that multiple sectors have an interest in green construction bolsters its future prospects.

Transportation

The outlook for green transportation can only be fully analysed in the context of broader phenomena such as population dispersion, migration patterns (including commuting) and general economic flows. Geographers tend to apply a "hinterland concept" when assessing the relationship between a population centre and the regions with which it entertains regular economic or other relations. Clearly, the longer the distances covered in an economy's supply chains, the greater its transportation needs (and the more it requires resources and generates pollution). The same applies when commuters face long daily journeys, reflecting an "extensive" spatial organisation. Macro-level responses at these levels might involve public mass transit systems or even urban infill policies directing further development to intra-mural brownfield sites instead to distant suburbs. Focusing on transportation modes exclusively without regard to more contextual factors necessarily limits understanding of improvement possibilities.

Otherwise, transportation vehicle sectors afford green business a number of opportunities. It is noteworthy that many companies' greening efforts in recent years have focused on vehicle technology – possibly because this is something that the private sector can control, as opposed to larger, more structural transportation infrastructure projects that usually necessitate government intervention (like the work being done to optimise traffic flows via "smart infrastructure" sensors and software). Above all, the transportation sector is a leading user of natural resources and producer of pollution – explaining why it is seen as the frontline for many green business initiatives.

Aviation

Flying is the mode of transportation that has received most criticism for its environmental footprint. Although it only accounts for a small percentage of all greenhouse gases at present (and despite the design of new energy-efficient aircraft), this proportion is expected to increase – in part because the gases planes emit in the upper atmosphere tend to have stronger effects. The commoditisation of flying for both business and leisure travellers means that passenger numbers have skyrocketed in recent years despite higher ticket prices resulting from fuel inflation and the generalisation of airport taxes. Airline sector profitability does not entirely reflect this trend, since in addition to funding rising fuel costs operators must also finance enormous fixed assets and regularly struggle to adjust their capacities to demand variations. Add to this the extreme competition affecting the sector since its general deregulation – plus the rise of discount airliners – and the picture is one of a business whose future appears anything but sustainable.

Railways

Like aviation, railways require significant upfront investment. Train itineraries are just as inflexible as planes, since they only offer "port-to-port" links and require users to organise further connections to their final destination. On the other hand, trains perform astronomically better in fuel efficiency and carbon emission terms, which may explain why the outlook for this sector is so much more positive.

Countries where the rail network is relatively underdeveloped are experiencing a small boom in this sector. On the one hand, trains are increasingly viewed as a more rational means to transport large passenger numbers. The idea is that many citizens will stop flying or driving if rail links are established, possibly using a hub system connecting intra-urban transport systems with inter-city fast train networks – the latter being a sector dominated by industrialists from countries already featuring integrated systems of this kind.

Note as well the strong move afoot to transfer freight traffic from road to rail, despite the latter mode's relative inflexibility. At a macro level, the shift would hugely reduce fuel consumption and carbon emissions (although provisions would still have to be made to transfer goods from freight depots to final destination). Trains, the earliest mode of motorised transportation, also appear to have the brightest future.

Shipping

In terms of the per kilometre cost of transporting a given volume of goods, shipping is just as efficient a mode of transportation as rail and therefore an attractive alternative. The problem, of course, lies in this mode's very inflexible infrastructure and the even greater fixed costs involved in building ocean-worthy vessels as well as port infrastructure. Shipping's inability to service the world's many landlocked destinations also undermines its universality, meaning that growth prospects in the sector, despite its comparatively low footprint, remain limited.

Still, some notable efforts are being made to further improve shipping's environmental performance. One involves "air lubrication" reducing friction between seawater and the ship's hull. Another involves improvements in propeller technology. A third innovation seeks to use energy storage devices to diversify a ship's power sources – being a further reminder of the manifold green business opportunities in batteries and other energy transmission systems.

Road

Nowhere is the battery logic more advanced than in the automotive sector – which can be subdivided into different categories, starting with freight and logistics, a sector responsible for a sizeable percentage of total global transport emissions (despite recent technological improvements). Above all, there is the passenger car sector, where several fully operative electrical (or at least hybrid) prototypes are already being widely marketed. The background to this transition is the fear of future fuel price raises and deteriorating driving conditions on increasingly congested networks – not to mention internal combustion vehicles' huge contribution to the emission of carbon dioxide and other gases (some of which have been proven to be carcinogenic). Under these conditions, the big question is why consumers' take-up of zero or low emission automobiles has not been quicker in fact.

At one level, the answer lies in the financial incentives required to induce a transition to modes of transportation that are less convenient. Incentives include punitive sanctions such as congestion charges and higher fuel and road taxes – but also positive measures such as subsidised public transportation. Policy varies widely, however, meaning that for most citizens, the advantage of foregoing passenger cars is not obvious given how high public transit fares still seem compared with the "free" solution of simply driving away in one's car. Of course, cars are anything but free – they cost a lot to buy, operate and maintain. The sector offers a further example of consumers ignoring the total costs associated with a certain habitat decision (car ownership, in this instance) and focusing instead on the immediate financial cost of the more environmentally friendly option – a cognitive problem felt at every level of green marketing.

Even when consumers have heard of greener driving systems, they usually possess little knowledge in the area – a confusion fed by fears about performance (speed, durability, comfort and safety). Then comes the barrier of price, since green cars cost more than non-green alternatives offering similar performance. This price differential is expected to last either until battery technologies become cheaper and more efficient, or until oil prices skyrocket to such a point that current petrol-based driving systems become prohibitively expensive. Lastly, there are fears about spare part stocks, and at a more fundamental level, the availability of electric recharging facilities. The sum total of these effects explains why despite all the publicity, green cars still account for such a small proportion of all passenger vehicles.

At the same time, the very fact that the sector is taking so long to develop might be viewed as an opportunity. As with any infant industry, timing is a key question. There are several reasons justifying this view. First the automotive industry and its supply chain are major employers, making their sustainable redesign a policy priority for many governments. Otherwise, rapid car use in the Global South is bound to produce certain very negative side effects, not only locally (smog, congestion on roads ill equipped for such traffic) but also globally (carbon dioxide emissions). This is worrying for bodies of global governance such as the European Union, spurring them to try and convince car manufacturers – in part, via tax incentives – to voluntarily lower new vehicles' carbon emissions.

Manufacturers are also reshaping this new framework, in part by expanding the offer of all-electric models and their enabling components. Other greening efforts involve the development of lightweight carbon fibre cars; driverless automobiles; and battery leasing arrangements that lower the surcharge consumers face when operating an electrical vehicle. Lastly, there is a concerted effort in some corners to establish fuel stations dispensing biodiesel made from vegetable oil. The sheer number of initiatives being fostered in this sector intimates that many more can be expected.

Bibliography

Greenbiz (2019), "State of Green Business" annual report, website: https://www.greenbiz.com/microsite/state-green-business

Klitkou, A. et al. (2019), From Waste to Value: Valorisation Pathways for Organic Waste in Circular Bioeconomies, Routledge.

Nidumolu, R. et al (2009), "Why sustainability is now the key driver of innovation", *Harvard Business Review*, www.hbr.org

Schendler, A. (2009), *Getting Green Done: Hard Truths from the Front Lines of the Sustainability Revolution*, PublicAffairs.

Williams, E. (2015), *Green Giants: How Smart Companies Turn Sustainability into Billion-Dollar Businesses*, Amacom.

9 Clean energy ventures

"Solar is great. They get a job, you get a tan"

ESSENTIAL SUMMARY

Previous chapters have discussed the many different ways in which ecological considerations affect business operations. Since organisations' limited capacities force them to prioritise the challenges they face, the question then becomes how companies should rank various environmental issues. Given the financial constraints weighing on all business activities, the issues most likely to receive managers' immediate attention are ones

(Continued)

that have a direct bearing on the bottom line. In green business, this often means energy supplies and pricing. That being the case, it is no surprise that the fortunes of the new clean energy sector dominate green business headlines.

The many millions of new "green jobs" that most analysts predict for the near future often refer to eco-efficient clean technology in general, covering a host of sectors. The present chapter, on the other hand, focuses specifically on sectors of activity responsible for the generation and distribution of renewable clean energy. What is exciting for green business is the likelihood that this sector might explode in the coming years as the energy crunch hits global business. Joining a sector just before it takes off is a fantastic opportunity – as exemplified by the fortunes of those who were lucky enough to start working with computers in the early 1980s.

Within the clean energy sector itself, a distinction should be made between new ventures and large existing companies. Each category has a different effect on the overall creation of green jobs – with larger companies' green initiatives often involving a simple reallocation of workers previously employed in other functions. Otherwise, larger firms will also have deeper pockets, placing them in a better position to survive the cash shortages that are endemic to the introduction phase of this like any other infant industry. Start-ups are more limited, on the other hand, if only because they rely solely on entrepreneurs' own resources or capital sourced from external fund providers like venture capitalists.

This argument can be turned around, however, since big companies' greater capital requirements often force them to seek funding from the financial markets, whose short-term focus generally means that new activities will have less time to justify themselves. Indeed, big energy companies may like trumpeting their devotion to clean energy but there is always a suspicion that this might be an exercise in greenwashing. Big companies also tend to have more institutionalised paradigms as well as significant sunk investments in the status quo, undermining their willingness to shift wholesale to radically disruptive new technologies. This is not to say that they do not have a major role to play in the new clean energy sector – but it does explain why start-ups have been such a driving force in this field so far.

Section I. Clean energy

In line with the green business principle that managers stand to benefit from greater knowledge of the physical environment within which they operate, it is appropriate for analysis of the clean energy sector to start with a review of the underlying science. This will involve a brief introduction to the generation and transmission of consumable energy, followed by a discussion of the factors driving the two key technologies in this new industrial revolution – solar and wind power.

Generation and transmission

All economic activity is predicated on an expenditure of energy that has been captured and re-directed in a way that creates a concentrated force. The animal (or human) forces driving pre-industrial economies drew their strength directly from food, via a slow and inefficient conversion process characterised by scant energy density. Hence the first Industrial Revolution, which began with James Watt's 1775 invention of the steam engine, powered by having combustibles like wood or coal generate steam that could then be used to turn pistons inside of a cylinder. The stroke action produced in this way concentrated kinetic energy capable of operating factory machinery – a classic example of the economic benefits of energy intensity.

Watt's steam engine had a major problem, however - it was relatively inefficient and generated a great deal of heat waste. Since then, the business world has been looking for new and better modes of power generation and transmission – often based on electrical solutions.

Scientists have long had a basic understanding of electricity, which occurs when subatomic particles subjected to electromagnetic fields generate electric charges whose movement creates a current that can be channelled as a power source. The main challenge was capturing these energy flows – an outcome most famously achieved in the late 19th century by Thomas Edison, best known for his invention of the electric light bulb but who also registered countless other patents, most notably for an electricity distribution system. This paved the way for the power grids upon which all societies have relied for more than a century now.

Clearly, Edison's electricity grid is not the only way of transmitting energy – as exemplified by the vast network of service stations distributing petrol for internal combustion engine-propelled automobiles, or the pipelines delivering the natural gas used in so many buildings today for heating or other purposes. Moreover, there is some question about the efficiency of the grid approach, given the enormous amount of energy wasted when electricity is transmitted over long distances in its customary "alternating current" form (with up to 40 percent being lost according to some calculations). The problem is that the uneven global dispersion of factor endowments such as oil means that energy is often produced at a great distance from where it is consumed. Moreover, there is every chance that transmission distances will increase in the future as renewable fuels – often sourced from sparsely populated locations including (for solar arrays) the Sahara, Gobi or Mojave deserts – account for a greater proportion of total energy production.

Another problem in energy supply is intermittency, a term that can mean different things. First, it is often difficult matching supplies to demand levels that can vary considerably on a seasonal and even hour-to-hour basis. Power companies often try to solve the imbalance between "baseline" and peak consumption by building added capacity in plants fired by conventional fuels and left in a "part-loaded" state of readiness. This is an expensive solution, although costs can be cut when smart grids are used to direct supplies on an as needs be basis; or if temporary energy surpluses are not wasted but stored. Second, where solar or wind power is concerned, these sources' intermittency means they must often be supplemented by conventional fuels usually generated in large scale power plants. These are few and far between, however, since each must be big enough to achieve economies of scale – a practical argument undermining many environmentalists' preference for micro-generation. All in all, the likelihood is that the current grid approach, despite its imperfections, will survive for many years still.

Innovation in this area has tended to focus on aspirations such as increasing electric lines' efficiency by investing in high-voltage, direct current; expanding portability via the miniaturisation of energy sources; and above all, enhancing energy storage technologies – explaining the tremendous interest at present in battery technology.

Current research in this latter sub-sector focuses on active materials such as lithium-ion that offer greater energy density and are capable of charging and discharging many times without losing too much power; super-sized batteries strong enough to run large automobiles (and even small electricity grids); and "distributed" or "flow" schemes that draw surplus energy accumulating in one section of a closed system before storing it elsewhere for later usage. Future research may involve "lithium metal-air" batteries whose energy intensity is as explosive as petrol; two-way transfers between idled electrical vehicles and municipal electricity grids; "ultracapacitor" devices; hydrogen fuel cells; or air compression techniques. The growth prospects for all of these technologies depend on whether they can be made feasible at a competitive cost – and on how quickly first mover companies can impose their in-house technology as industry standard.

Solar and wind – the main renewables

It is important to specify that countries' variable endowment in sun and wind – far and away the two leading clean energy sectors – makes it hard to generalise about a global renewables market. Instead, the picture is one of differentiated national performances. Certain aspects of this new business have clearly globalised, specifically renewables equipment manufacturing, whose industrialisation has followed a relatively standard development path. Yet even this one activity is affected by climate variations since entrepreneurs located in countries with a particular natural resource will have an additional incentive to invest in a technology taking advantage of whatever factor is abundant locally. Moreover, above and beyond these upstream considerations, the clean technology sector is also associated with a number of downstream competencies, namely new equipment installation and grid connection. Such activities necessarily entail a local presence, however, explaining the frequent adoption of vertical integration strategies involving a large global equipment maker (of solar panels, of wind turbines) who then acquires small local installers. The renewables business is both international and domestic.

Solar

The solar and wind sectors have variable prospects, however. Solar, for instance, has historically attracted enormous investor attention, if only because the sun theoretically produces sufficient power to cover all of the Earth's total energy needs. Expected advances in solar technology have also started driving down the sector's production costs – to the extent that certain manufacturers have already started to realise substantial economies of scale, sparking a virtuous circle between lower cost and higher demand.

Solar power refers to both silicon-based photovoltaic (PV) cells that convert sunlight into electric current; and thermal captors, where "heliostat" mirrors collect heat and use it for a variety of purposes, including to make steam that can then be used to drive turbine generators. From a technological perspective, progress in this area involves materials or designs that store heat or convert electricity more

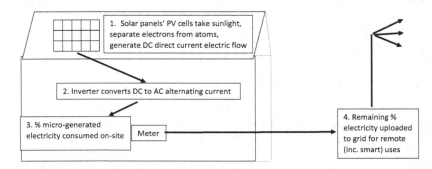

Figure 9.1 Solar Panel and Grid.

efficiently. Much attention has also been focused on parabolic systems that track the sun as it travels across the sky. In market terms, the key differentiation is between small home or commercial building installations and huge solar arrays that increasingly use concentrator technologies to magnify the sun's effects. Target customers differ in each of these categories, with smaller installations being of interest to homeowners and developers (especially where the structures concerned feature sufficient weight-bearing roof space) and larger arrays being more of a focus for industrialists and utilities (Figure 9.1).

In the absence of government action, the solar sector's take-off will depend on two factors: whether conventional fuel prices rise enough to spark a widespread search for substitute energy sources; and whether technology advances sufficiently to make solar competitive. To a large extent, this latter condition has already been fulfilled, due in part to knowledge spillovers from other industries (like semiconductors) mobilising similar skills sets – with the nano-technology used to imprint memory on computer hard drives involving a knowledge similar to the one applied to thin-film solar cells. This synergy may help to explain the arrival of Silicon Valley computer firms in the budding solar sector.

Lastly, note the widespread green business consensus that global installed solar capacity is destined to rise in the years to come. What is unclear is how future growth will break down between smaller building-specific solar units and large-scale solar arrays. The distinction is crucial since there is no reason to expect the construction and utilities sectors to enjoy the same success. Quite the contrary, whereas land use and financial constraints are likely to slow the small solar sector in the absence of weatherisation subsidies, there is every chance that wholesale renewables utilities will attract investment as traditional fuel sources deplete. This intimates that the focus of the new solar sector will tilt more towards mega-projects, increasingly located in the world's sunniest regions (to wit, its deserts). Typically, the main hurdle for projects of this nature is capital expenditure, relating as much to the distribution of the electricity being produced as to the actual generation equipment. This need for a substantial upfront outlay favours large providers with deep pockets and explains some of the recent consolidations that have rattled the infant solar industry. The question then becomes when the sector will stabilise to provide steady returns attracting further players.

Wind

The situation for wind power is similar to solar insofar as both currently account for at best a few percentage points in most countries' energy mix; both are currently experiencing impressive growth rates; and both continue to face a number of stumbling blocks. Windmill technology has been around for thousands of years and is based on the simple idea that strong winds pushing blades attached to a tower create mechanical energy that a generator converts into electrical energy. Improvements can always be made in different components' costs and performance, with an estimated half of wind turbines' total capital investment involving infrastructure (foundations and cables); one quarter the tower and turbine; and one quarter the gearbox and associated parts. It is worth noting that asides from the cables connecting turbines to the grid (an aspect requiring some understanding of electronics), the primary skill set required by wind technology is mechanical in nature – a knowledge base that is well established and widely dispersed worldwide. Thus, success in this sector is predicated less on advanced science and more on financial and human capital (i.e. the need for trained installers). This makes wind power technology less esoteric – and more widespread internationally – than solar.

At the same time, there are serious questions about the maximum potential of wind power, if only because of small installations' poor cost/benefit ratio. Wind investments can only be justified if the chosen locations both benefit from strong average speed winds and are sufficiently close to users to avoid the loss of too much energy during transmission. But it is rare that perfect wind conditions exist in the municipal areas where most energy is consumed, if only because such habitats have historically been specifically chosen because they offer protection from the elements. The net effect has been a certain disaffection in recent years for micro-wind projects and a preference for locating massive wind farms on locales renowned for tempestuous weather conditions.

Having said that, wind farms located on urban peripheries or in the countryside also face numerous obstacles, starting with frequent opposition from authorities who hesitate to give planning permission for projects that will alter local scenery, kill birds, etc. A distinction should be made between complaints from residents who do not require the extra power and are unhappy that their neighbourhood is being appropriated to serve distant, energy-wasteful populations, versus NIMBY (not in my backyard) interests who consume great quantities of energy but simply refuse to have it produced locally. The political balance of power between these and other constituencies differs globally and goes some way towards explaining the varying potential for wind arrays in different regional markets.

Other, more technical factors include the advantage of building very tall structures that necessarily require deep foundations, an engineering feat that increases wind projects' upfront costs and makes the sector generally more reliant on external fund providers such as banks or investors. The intermittency of wind and frequent lack of correlation between different sites' wind speeds means that developers are often advised to build a multitude of arrays at a distance from one another, with stormy conditions on one location counter-balancing calm weather at another. This too raises overall costs, since each site will require its own grid connections and also because the project as a whole requires a larger land purchase.

Despite these constraints, recent years have witnessed a number of large-scale wind farm investments globally. Of course, the big entrepreneurs generally driving such mega-projects usually possess the relational networks enabling the fund-raising they require. This may explain why large corporate renewables divisions appear to be taking over from small- and medium-sized enterprises (SMEs) as the main drivers in both wind and solar. The relationship between a company's size and its access to funding is a key factor in determining the trajectory of a new green business sector like clean energy.

Section II. Funding the clean energy transition

Like all infant industries, clean energy has been hampered by high start-up costs, insufficient economies of scale and immature technology. Unlike most earlier industrial revolutions, however, the sector's take-off phase had the bad luck of coinciding with a global funding crisis (being the huge rise in public debt that came out of the 2008 credit crunch). One of the effects has been to limit the amount of capital available to green entrepreneurs. This is a severe handicap in a new industry – external capital is the lifeblood of start-ups that do not yet benefit from sufficient demand to be self-sustaining. In analytical terms, the lesson is that the outlook for this and other new sectors can only be judged accurately in the light of the financial and macro-economic conditions surrounding their birth.

State support

Clean energy's first funding channel – in visibility if not volume terms – is comprised of government investments and incentives coming in the form of grants, subsidies, production tax credits or cheap loans. Although many countries have devised packages supporting SMEs' actions in new green sectors, larger companies with their streamlined procedures are generally in a better position to apply for public funds. SMEs would be hard pressed to lead projects on a large scale, with their involvement generally being limited to a subcontractor's role. Having said that, SMEs are often in a better position to benefit from the much smaller micro-investment packages that many local authorities have started to develop worldwide (community power generation schemes, etc.).

It is unclear how big conglomerates analyse the financial aspects of their own clean energy initiatives since projects of this kind are often aimed at improving the performance of their other business lines. Hence the idea that large companies' return on investment calculations might be improved if their green activities were treated as standalone profit centres. Note that governmental influence on green finance is not limited to direct funding alone, since legislative decisions (like so-called "renewables obligations") taken with a view towards achieving particular clean energy goals will also impact the corporate bottom line. All in all, clean energy funding is more than a series of ad hoc financial transactions and can only be analysed accurately within a broader regime.

Private finance

The second clean energy funding channel – private finance - is also influenced by the state's actions since investors interested in a new industry will clearly be somewhat reassured if their government also commits strongly to it. This is particularly true for financial investors such as hedge funds or private equity firms who might otherwise be daunted by the low margins characterising industries like clean energy that are still in their infant phase. Note also that stock market enthusiasm for clean energy can vary sharply from one quarter to another, often due to irrational market sentiment. Given its evolving profile, the sector is subject to greater market volatility than most of its older counterparts. Of course, short-term market sentiment will be less of a factor for those investors who are more focused on long-term industrial outcomes. What this reveals is the impossibility of analysing green funding behaviour without understanding the specific goals of the parties involved.

The rise of "socially responsible investing" (SRI) as an asset class has created a whole framework for green investment – albeit one that often has greater relevance to established companies' energy efficiency efforts than to new ventures' capital needs. SRI varies greatly internationally in market percentage terms. Today, most large companies are screened to see whether their practices fit a given SRI group's requirements. This has underpinned the establishment of a number of well-known "screened indexes" such as the Dow Jones Sustainability World Index and the FTSE4Good Index. Companies listed by these indexes are deemed to conduct themselves in a sustainable manner, usually based on their triple bottom reporting or compliance with Global Reporting Initiative (GRI) guidelines.

Similarly, ethical rating agencies and non-governmental organisations such as CERES, the Carbon Disclosure Project or the United Nations Environmental Programme (UNEP) work alongside today's investors to pressure companies into improving their environmental performance, governance and disclosure. The idea here is that full understanding of a company's financial potential is only possible if its environmental activities are also taken into account. Expressed in financial terms, this means that companies that are attractive to investors due to their high environmental governance standards and low legal liabilities will find it easier to attract funding and lower their overall cost of capital. The complication is that some investor groups can get more excited about clean energy opportunities than others. The risk is that this inconsistency can spark further price bubbles, adding to market volatility and dampening overall investor enthusiasm. Like other sectors, clean energy is not always characterised by rational thinking alone.

Because the diversification of funding sources spreads risk and alleviates the kind of investor disaffection from which an infant industry such as clean energy tends to suffer – a serious hurdle given the massive sums needed to meet global (clean) energy needs – there has been a recent trend towards co-investment projects combining government monies with bank funding and private equity. At the same time, some financial institutions have made a strategic choice to commit to clean energy and are purposefully seeking to expand their presence in this sector. The vehicle that bankers clearly prefer in this area is asset financing; far behind this, the sector's second leading source of finance comes from initial public offerings and assimilated capital market issues.

Last but not least, a comparatively lesser source of clean energy funding is venture capital (VC) – a variant of private equity finance of particular interest to entrepreneurs. Since the computer revolution of the 1980s, the relationship between high-tech start-ups and venture capitalists has been widely hailed as a key driver of innovation in the modern era. VC firms invest their or their customers' funds in small companies in the hope these will turn into the Microsofts or Apples of tomorrow. The problem is that relatively few solar start-ups have qualified for introduction to a stock exchange, which is how venture capitalists usually make their profits. Clean energy's lengthy introduction phase means that the sector is of greater interest to long-term investors interested in positioning themselves in the industries of the future as opposed to short-term speculators more focused on immediate returns. This compartmentalises the sector's investor base and influences green entrepreneurs' funding quests. It also means that in finance as in so many other areas, the economic reasoning driving green business is aligned with its seminal ecological principles.

Bibliography

Bloomberg NEF Renewable Energy website: https://about.bnef.com/blog/

Brown, M. (2001), "Market failures and barriers as a basis for clean energy policies", *Energy Policy*, Volume 29, Issue 14, pp. 1197–1207.

International Renewable Energy Agency website: https://www.irena.org/ourwork/Knowledge-Data-Statistics/Data-Statistics

Pernick, R. (2007), *The Clean Tech Revolution: The Next Big Growth and Investment Opportunity*, Harper-Collins, New York.

Seba, T. (2010), *Solar Trillions: 7 Market and Investment Opportunities in the Emerging Clean-Energy Economy*, Tony Seba, San Francisco.

Index

agriculture/agribusiness 3, 5, 10, 15, 18, 22, 29, 32, 36, 72, 88, 90–2
air quality (smog) 8, 28, 38, 45, 97
asset financing 109

balanced scorecard 58, 67
best practice 60, 66
biodegradable 9, 38, 66
biodiversity 24, 45, 65–6
biofuel 90
biomass 10, 24
biomimicry 9, 65
biophilic 93
biosphere 32
brand tribes 84

carbon (emission) trading 47, 50
certification 25, 59, 69–70
Clean Development Mechanism 47
clean energy 47, 99–109
climate change 20–1, 24–5, 28, 30–1, 47, 61, 70
closed loop 65–6, 74
code of conduct 56, 60
combined heat and power (CHP) 93
corporate (social) responsibility 7, 52
cradle-to-cradle 65–6

dead zones 10, 37
deep ecology 4, 5
demography 3, 16, 81
disassembly 56, 66, 74
disclosure 59–60, 108

eco-efficiency 9, 63–8, 70, 72, 74, 100
eco-labelling 59, 61–2, 84

ecological imperative iii, viii, 4, 7, 12–13, 21, 30, 72, 79
ecological justice 45
ecological thinking 3, 6–7, 68
ecological value 44–5
ecology 3–5, 8, 68, 90
ecosystem 9, 24–5, 33, 35, 37, 42–3, 45, 64
embedded inputs 36, 56–7, 64, 90
emerging economies (Global South) 3, 12, 16, 19, 25, 30, 47, 72, 89, 91, 97
energy density 101–2
energy distribution 17
energy elasticity 26
energy intensity 16–17, 91, 101–2
environmental disasters 5–8, 28, 38, 43
environmental footprint 11, 33, 36–7, 47, 55–8, 65, 68–70, 72, 83, 93, 95–6
environmentalism 2, 4, 6, 7, 11–12, 15, 41, 44, 56, 60, 75–6, 82–3
environmental management system (EMS) 56–8, 67
(environmental) reputation 11, 34, 59, 69, 71, 73, 82, 84–5, 93
e-waste 38, 67
externalities 11, 32, 34, 45–6

finite 3, 15–16, 19, 21–2, 24, 42–3
food miles 72, 90
fossil (conventional) fuels 10, 16, 18, 20–1, 24, 29, 102, 104
free ride 11, 33, 45, 48

genetically modified (GM) organisms 5, 90
global governance 33, 97
globalisation 7, 16, 38, 89, 103
Global Reporting Initiative (GRI) 57, 60, 108
global warming 10, 19, 25, 30–1, 35, 82, 91
green chemistry 9, 35
green finance 107
greenhouse gases/effect 10, 20–1, 30, 36, 47, 49, 56, 58, 73, 95
green marketing 7, 74–86, 97
green (premium) pricing 79, 81–2
green promotion 84–5
Green Revolution 5, 88–9
greenwash 78, 86, 100
grid 15, 67, 101–6

habitat 24, 44, 92, 97, 105
halo effect 79
heat waste 9, 101
hinterland 94

industrial ecology 68
inertia 15, 43, 54
inputs 9, 14, 23, 27, 32, 36, 38, 44, 57, 64–9, 71–2, 81
intermittency 34, 102, 106
international business iii, 12, 30, 41, 44

license to operate 50
life cycle (assessment) 9, 23, 56, 58, 61, 65–6, 69, 79–80, 82
lightweighting 66, 82
LOHAS 79

market failure 45, 47
materialism 44
metrics 56–8, 61–2
micro-generation 17, 102
multinational enterprise (MNE) 12, 30, 48, 72, 84, 90

natural capitalism 8, 42
natural resources iii, 2, 15, 23, 42–4, 53, 95
non-governmental organisation (NGO) 24, 59, 108
non-product output (NPO) 32, 61, 70–1

organic 9, 20, 29, 37, 80, 82, 90

photosynthesis 9, 10
planned obsolescence 22, 32, 64
polluter pays principle 46
pollution (generation, abatement, mitigation, etc.) 9, 11, 15, 21, 24, 27–8, 30–8, 44–6, 48, 55–6, 58, 61, 68, 70, 72, 76, 91, 94, 95
precautionary principle 2, 32, 60
public goods 42

quality 5, 9, 32, 38, 57, 61, 64, 68, 70, 81

race to the bottom 12, 30
recycling/reverse logistics 10, 22, 32, 55–6, 58, 65, 68, 73–4, 81, 83, 89, 92
regime arbitrage 48
relative price 10, 89
renewable (energy) 20, 22, 38, 47, 65, 100, 102–3, 106–7
reporting group 57, 59–61
resilience 35, 90
resource depletion 3, 14–26, 44, 76, 89
resource husbandry 65, 90
retrofitting 93–4
right-sizing 70, 73

self-interest 41–2, 55, 77, 80, 85
sequestering 30, 93
small and medium-sized enterprises (SMEs) 60, 83, 106–7
smart grid 67, 102
social ecology 4, 5
socially responsible investing 108
social marketing 7, 76–7
soil 4, 10, 31–2, 36–7, 60
solar array 102, 104
solar radiation 8, 10
stakeholders 56, 58–60, 71, 84
stewardship 24–5, 44, 61, 73
stressor 33
sunk investments 11, 43, 64
supply chain 16, 23, 38, 69, 72, 90–1, 94, 97
sustainability 16, 24–5, 33, 37, 42–3, 47, 49, 52–3, 55, 58–60, 62, 64, 69, 83, 85, 90–1, 95, 97, 108
sustainable development 7

throughput 70
toxicity 34–5, 57, 60, 67
tragedy of the commons (c.f. Garrett Hardin) 6, 42
triple bottom line 58, 60, 108

upfront costs (initial outlay) 11, 82, 95, 105–6
upgradeability 66
urban sprawl 90

value chain 27, 32, 42, 57, 62, 66–72, 74
venture capital 100, 109

waste 6, 9, 14, 17, 21, 29, 32–5, 38, 49, 65–8, 70–1, 73, 80–1, 83, 101
water (quality, etc.) 5, 8, 10, 20, 24, 31, 33–4, 37, 54, 58, 60–1, 88, 91–2

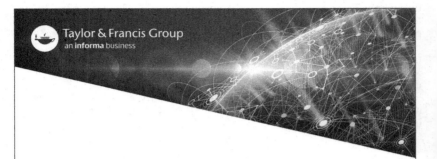

Printed in the United States
by Baker & Taylor Publisher Services